Grammar Practice Workbook

GRADE 4

Requests for permission to make copies of any part of the work should be submitted through our Permissions website at https://customercare.hmhco.com/contactus/Permissions.html or mailed to Houghton Mifflin Harcourt Publishing Company, Attn: Rights Compliance and Analysis, 9400 Southpark Center Loop, Orlando, Florida 32819-8647.

Printed in the U.S.A.

ISBN   978-0-358-24501-8

12 13 14   0909   28 27 26 25 24

450884821   A B C D E F G

Grade 4

Contents

Simple and Complete Subjects and Predicates

A sentence expresses a complete thought that contains a **simple subject** and a **simple predicate**.

A **subject** is the naming part of the sentence that tells who or what and is usually a noun.

A **predicate** is the action part of the sentence that tells what the subject does or did and always contains a verb.

> **Nancy baked** a cake. (*Nancy* is the simple subject, *baked* is the simple predicate.)

> **Identify the subject and predicate in each sentence.**

1. Kevin finished his homework. _____

2. Susan ate her lunch. _____

3. The firefighters extinguished the fire. _____

4. The deer ran across the road. _____

5. The students worked hard on their projects. _____

6. The team played well. _____

7. The teacher graded the homework. _____

8. Carol drove to the store. _____

9. The birds flew high in the sky. _____

10. The girl cried after she fell. _____

11. The chorus sang a beautiful song. _____

12. The principal read the announcements. _____

> **Revisit a piece of your writing. Edit the draft to make sure all subjects and predicates are used correctly.**

Name _____

Compound Subjects and Predicates

A sentence has a **compound subject** when there is more than one subject. It has a **compound predicate** when it has more than one predicate. Sometimes sentences can have both a compound subject and a compound predicate.

Joe and Kate had lunch in the cafeteria. (Compound subject)

The musician **sang, played the drums, and danced** on stage. (Compound predicate)

Jim and Patrick swam and rode their bikes together. (Compound subject *and* compound predicate)

> **Identify whether the sentence has a compound subject, a compound predicate, or both.**

1. Skiing and snowboarding are two winter sports in the Olympics.

   _____

2. Bobby delivered newspapers and mowed lawns over the summer.

   _____

3. Tim and his friends started a writing club. _____

4. The teacher and the students ran and played outside.

   _____

5. When they got to school, Danny and Ethan finished their reading and worked

   on their math. _____

> **Revisit a piece of your writing. Edit the draft to make sure all compound subjects and predicates are used correctly.**

Subject-Verb Agreement

A **subject** is the naming part of a simple or compound sentence that tells who or what. Subjects are usually nouns.

A **predicate** is the action part of the sentence that tells what the subject does or did and always contains a verb.

Verbs in the present tense have two forms. The correct form to use depends on the subject of the sentence.

Add -s to the verb when the noun in the subject is singular, unless the subject is *I*.

Do not add -s to the verb when the noun in the subject is plural.

> **Kara** serves the volleyball.
> *Kara* is the simple subject, *serves* is the simple predicate, add -s to *serve* because *Kara* is a singular noun.
>
> **The players** serve the volleyball.
> *The players* is the simple subject, *serve* is the simple predicate, do not add -s because *players* is plural.

> Underline the verb in the parentheses that agrees with its subject.

1. My cat (purr, purrs) when I pet her.

2. They (want, wants) another pet.

3. Dogs (like, likes) to play fetch and cats (love, loves) to play with toys.

4. He (share, shares) his lunch with his friend everyday.

5. The kids (laugh, laughs) when the principal (tell, tells) jokes.

> Revisit a piece of your writing. Edit the draft to make sure subject-verb agreement is used correctly.

Review Parts of a Sentence

Complete sentences are made up of a subject and a predicate. The **simple subject** is the noun that is the focus of the sentence. The complete subject is made up of all the words that tell who or what is doing the action in the sentence. A **compound subject** is made up of two or more subjects joined by a coordinating conjunction such as *and* or *or*.

The **simple predicate** is the verb that tells what the subject does or is. The complete predicate is made up of all the words that tell what the subject is or does. A **compound predicate** is made up of two or more predicates joined by a coordinating conjunction such as *and, or, but,* and *so*.

> **Underline the complete subject for each sentence and double underline the complete predicate.**

1. The wolf howled through the night.

2. Jerry bought us a pizza for dinner.

3. The students presented their projects.

4. We cheered on the home team.

5. Teachers grade many papers each day.

> **Revisit a piece of your writing. Edit the draft to make sure subject-verb agreement is used correctly.**

Connect to Writing: Using Sentences with Subject-Verb Agreement

> **Read the selection and choose the best answer to each question.**

Read the following paragraph about watching a football game. Look for any revisions that should be made. Then answer the questions that follow.

(1) Yesterday, we watch the homecoming football game. (2) My sister wanted to sit close to the cheerleaders. (3) I wanted to sit by the concession stand. (4) My mom and dad will want to sit closer to the band. (5) So, we decided to compromise and sit in the middle section of the bleachers.

1. Which statement has a verb that is written in the wrong tense?

   A. Yesterday, we watch the homecoming football game.

   B. My sister wanted to sit close to the cheerleaders.

   C. I wanted to sit by the concession stand.

   D. So, we decided to compromise and sit in the middle section of the bleachers.

2. What change should be made to sentence 4?

   A. It should be written in the past tense.

   B. It should be written in the present tense.

   C. It should be written in the future tense.

   D. Make no change.

> **What kind of sports or other events do you like to watch? Write two or three sentences about it.**

_____

_____

_____

_____

_____

Declarative and Interrogative Sentences

A **declarative sentence** is a statement and ends with a period.

An **interrogative sentence** asks a question, and it ends with a question mark.

> Jim went to the play. (declarative)
> What time does the game start? (interrogative)

▷ **Identify each as a declarative or interrogative sentence.**

1. My favorite flavor of ice cream is chocolate. _____

2. Can you come to my party? _____

3. Where did you get your coat? _____

4. I am going to the movies. _____

5. He has red hair. _____

6. Will you help me find my keys? _____

7. Jasmine draws with colored pencils. _____

8. Why did Ross leave early? _____

9. How will we get to the science museum? _____

10. When did Mariel start taking violin lessons? _____

▷ **Revisit a piece of your writing. Edit the draft to make sure interrogative and declarative sentences are used correctly.**

Imperative and Exclamatory Sentences

An **imperative sentence** is a command and is usually punctuated with a period.

An **exclamatory sentence** shows strong feeling and ends with an exclamation point. The exclamation point is used to highlight a strong feeling.

You must do your homework. (imperative)

I can't believe they lost the game! (exclamatory)

▶ **Identify each as an imperative or exclamatory sentence.**

1. Don't forget that you have to clean the fishtank. _____

2. I am so excited about my party! _____

3. I can't wait for the concert to start! _____

4. Explain why you can't find your books. _____

5. His dog just ran away! _____

6. Turn in your homework today. _____

7. You may not talk during the test. _____

8. We just won the championship game! _____

9. Hang your coats before you come into the classroom. _____

10. Put all recyclables in the blue and green bins. _____

▶ **Revisit a piece of your writing. Edit the draft to make sure imperative and exclamatory sentences are used correctly.**

Identify Kinds of Sentences

A **declarative sentence** is a statement and ends with a period.

An **interrogative sentence** asks a question, and it ends with a question mark.

An **imperative sentence** is a command and is usually punctuated with a period.

An **exclamatory sentence** shows strong feeling and ends with an exclamation point.

> Identify each sentence as declarative, interrogative, imperative, or exclamatory.

1. How old are you? _____

2. I am so happy to see you! _____

3. You must eat your dinner before you have dessert. _____

4. Walk in the hallway. _____

5. Do you like art or music class better? _____

6. The sun is bright today. _____

7. They went to the museum. _____

8. Happy Birthday! _____

9. Do not leave until the teacher tells you to. _____

10. I will wait for you outside the bookstore. _____

> Revisit a piece of your writing. Edit the draft to make sure all sentence types are used correctly.

Review Kinds of Sentences

A **declarative sentence** is a statement and ends with a period.

An **interrogative sentence** asks a question, and it ends with a question mark.

An **imperative sentence** is a command and is usually punctuated with a period.

An **exclamatory sentence** shows strong feeling and ends with an exclamation point.

> **Rewrite each sentence to make it the type indicated in parentheses.**

1. He is wearing a green shirt. (interrogative) _____

2. He is taking the trash outside. (imperative) _____

3. We need to find our lost dog. (exclamatory) _____

4. Sit quietly during the show. (declarative) _____

5. The other team won! (interrogative) _____

> **Revisit a piece of your writing. Edit the draft to make sure all sentence types are used correctly.**

Connect to Writing: Using Different Kinds of Sentences

> **Read the selection and choose the best answer to each question.**

Read the following paragraph about going to a friend's birthday party. Look for any revisions that should be made. Then answer the questions that follow.

(1) On Saturday, Dana is having her birthday party. (2) I'm so excited. (3) Do you think they will have games! (4) My mom is going to drop me off at 4 o'clock. (5) I hope we all have a great time!

1. Which statement does not end with the correct punctuation mark?

    A. On Saturday, Dana is having her birthday party.

    B. I'm so excited.

    C. My mom is going to drop me off at 4 o'clock.

    D. I hope we all have a great time!

2. What change should be made in sentence 3?

    A. It should written with a question mark.

    B. It should be written with a period.

    C. It should have a subject.

    D. Make no change.

> **Write about a birthday you remember. Be sure to include each type of sentence in your writing.**

_____

_____

_____

_____

Sentence Fragments

A **sentence fragment** is a group of words that does not tell a complete thought and lacks a subject, a predicate, or both.

The school bus. (fragment; missing predicate)
Went to the concert. (fragment; missing subject)

▶ **Identify if the sentence is complete or a fragment, then identify what is missing from each fragment — the subject or the predicate.**

1. The car door. _____

2. School started late because the roads were icy. _____

3. Going to the store. _____

4. The picture was in a frame. _____

5. The circus elephants. _____

▶ **Revisit a piece of your writing. Edit the draft to make sure sentence fragments are corrected.**

Run-On Sentences

A **run-on sentence** is a sentence that has two complete thoughts, or sentences, that run into each other without appropriate punctuation or a conjunction.

> Ann wanted a new car she got a second job. (run-on sentence)

To fix a run-on sentence, **add punctuation and a capital letter**.

> Ann wanted a new car. She got a second job.

OR

Add a comma and a conjunction.

> Ann wanted a new car, so she got a second job.

▶ **Correct the following run-on sentences by adding punctuation and a capital letter, or by forming a compound sentence by adding a comma and a conjunction.**

1. Today is warm and sunny we will go to the swimming pool.
   Add a comma and a conjunction.

   _____

2. Beth has always enjoyed country music I don't like it very much.
   Add punctuation and a capital letter.

   _____

3. I called my older brother to pick me up he couldn't leave practice.
   Add a comma and a conjunction.

   _____

4. The dancers at the show were great they weren't very good last year.
   Add punctuation and a capital letter.

   _____

5. Brandon went to the dentist today he didn't have any cavities.
   Add a comma and a conjunction.

   _____

Writing Complete Sentences

A **complete sentence** tells a complete thought and has a subject and a predicate.

The dog at the door. (fragment)

I was thirsty, I made some tea. (comma splice)

He went to the store he needed milk. (run-on)

The students returned their books to the library. (complete sentence)

> Identify each as a fragment, run-on, comma splice, or complete sentence. For fragments, run-ons, or comma splices, rewrite as complete sentences.

1. Patrick needs to take piano lessons but he thinks he plays well.

   _____

2. Hit the ball. _____

3. I woke up late, I didn't have breakfast this morning.

   _____

4. Fish and frogs live in the pond. _____

5. Our class won the contest we had lunch with the principal.

   _____

> Revisit a piece of your writing. Edit the draft to make sure complete sentences are written correctly.

Review Fragments and Run-On Sentences

A **sentence fragment** is a group of words that does not tell a complete thought.

A **run-on sentence** is a sentence that has two complete thoughts, or sentences, that run into each other.

Played well. (fragment; The team played well.)

The shoes were real leather they were expensive. (run-on; The shoes were real leather. They were expensive.)

> **Correct and rewrite each fragment and run-on sentence below. Add sentence parts where appropriate.**

1. At the park.

_____

2. The kittens.

_____

3. She had to do the laundry she also had to wash the dishes.

_____

4. The rehearsal begins at 3:00 P.M. we should hurry.

_____

5. The basketball team.

_____

> **Revisit a piece of your writing. Edit the draft to make sure fragments and run-on sentences are corrected.**

Connect to Writing: Using Complete Sentences

▶ **Read the selection and choose the best answer to each question.**
Read the following paragraph about eating a meal at Grandma's house. Look for any revisions that should be made. Then answer the questions that follow.

(1) Sunday afternoon. (2) Grandma always makes roast and noodles. (3) Her pies. (4) My cousins and I help clean up the dishes. (5) We want to go there next Sunday.

1. Which statement is not a complete sentence?

   A. Sunday afternoon.

   B. Grandma always makes roast and noodles.

   C. My cousins and I help clean up the dishes.

   D. Make no changes.

2. What change should be made in sentence 3?

   A. It should written with a subject.

   B. Make no changes.

   C. It should be written as a complete sentence.

   D. It should be written with an adjective.

▶ **Write about one of your favorite meals or family feasts. Make certain to write your story in complete sentences.**

_____

_____

_____

_____

Compound Sentences

A **compound sentence** is a sentence that has two simple sentences joined by a comma and a connecting word, such as *and*, *or*, *but*, or *so*.

John packed his clothes. He started thinking about summer camp.

John packed his clothes, **and** he started thinking about summer camp.

▷ **Create a compound sentence by combining the two simple sentences below with connecting words (and, or, but, so).**

1. David does not like chicken. He eats hamburgers.

_____

2. Liam likes video games. He does not like to pay for video games.

_____

3. Would you like to go to the movies? Would you rather stay home tonight?

_____

4. Nancy must pass her test. She will not be able to go to the movies.

_____

5. The girls were painting pictures of flowers. Mary spilled the paint.

_____

▷ **Revisit a piece of your writing. Edit the draft to make sure compound sentences are written correctly.**

Complex Sentences

> A **compound sentence** is a sentence that has two simple sentences joined by a comma and a connecting word, such as *and*, *or*, *but*, or *so*.
>
> A **complex sentence** is a sentence made up of a simple sentence and a clause joined with a subordinating conjunction such as *because*, *although*, *until*, *if*, or *since*.
>
>   Compound sentence: The house was destroyed in the fire, but the whole family was saved.
>
>   Complex sentence: The teacher returned the homework because she noticed the student forgot the second page.

▶ **Identify which of the following sentences are compound and which are complex.**

1. The girls would plan a sleepover, or they would plan a swim party. _____

2. Sophie slept late, but she made it to school on time. _____

3. Eli played football, so his brother played soccer. _____

4. I'll go to the store since I have no bread. _____

5. After they finished studying, Amber and Mindy went to the movies. _____

6. Because it was raining, the tennis match was called off. _____

7. He is going to the dance, so he has to buy a new suit. _____

8. Noah is studying because he has a test tomorrow. _____

9. Since he was not invited, Mark is not going to the party. _____

10. I took a French class, and my friend took a Spanish class. _____

▶ **Revisit a piece of your writing. Edit the draft to make sure complex sentences are written correctly.**

Commas in Compound Sentences

In a **compound sentence**, two independent sentences are joined by a comma which is used before the conjunction. Conjunctions include: *and, or, but, so*

Two independent sentences:
I don't want to eat my vegetables. I do want ice cream after dinner. (but)
Compound sentence:
I don't want to eat my vegetables, but I do want to have ice cream after dinner.

> **Using the two independent sentences, form a compound sentence by adding a comma and the conjuction given in parentheses.**

1. They got to the concert early. They got really good seats. (and)

   _____

2. It was getting dark. We thought we should go home. (so)

   _____

3. She didn't want to go to the doctor. She went anyway. (but)

   _____

4. Would you like to go to the game today? Would you rather go to the movies? (or)

   _____

5. Jessica's friends were busy. She went on a bike ride by herself. (so)

   _____

> **Revisit a piece of your writing. Edit the draft to make sure commas in compound sentences are written correctly.**

Review Compound and Complex Sentences

In a **compound sentence**, two independent sentences are joined by a comma which is used before the conjunction. Conjunctions include: *and*, *or*, *but*, *so*

A **complex sentence** is made up of a simple sentence and a dependent clause joined with a subordinating conjunction, such as *because, although, until, if,* or *since*.

Compound sentence: John finished his homework, so he was able to play computer games.

Complex sentence: Since you need some help painting, I'll come over this afternoon.

▶ **Identify each sentence below as compound or complex.**

1. We need go to the bank because we need some money. _____

2. Since it was raining, we left the park. _____

3. I didn't study enough, so I didn't pass my test. _____

4. I thought I remembered where I left my keys, but I still can't find them. _____

5. Mom made a delicious dinner, and Aunt Teri brought pie for dessert. _____

▶ **Revisit a piece of your writing. Edit the draft to make sure compound and complex sentences are written correctly.**

Connect to Writing: Using Compound and Complex Sentences

> **Read the selection and choose the best answer to each question.**

Read the following paragraph about going on a field trip. Look for any revisions that should be made. Then answer the questions that follow.

(1) Tomorrow, we are going on a field trip. (2) Tomorrow, we are going to the zoo. (3) There will be elephants and giraffes at the zoo. (4) There will be so many great things to see!

1. Which two sentences can be combined to form a compound or complex sentence? Circle both answer choices.

   A. Tomorrow, we are going on a field trip.

   B. Tomorrow, we are going to the zoo.

   C. There will be elephants and giraffes at the zoo.

   D. There will be so many great things to see!

2. What changes could be made in sentences 3 and 4, if any?

   A. They should be written as questions.

   B. They should be combined.

   C. Make no changes.

   D. They should both have exclamation points.

> **Write about a time you went on a field trip or a family trip. Make sure to use compound and/or complex sentences properly.**

_____

_____

_____

_____

Capitalizing Historical Events and Documents

A **proper noun** is a word that names a particular person, place, or thing, and begins with a capital letter. The names of historical periods, events, and documents are proper nouns and should be capitalized, too. Remember, common nouns are not capitalized.

George Washington was our first president.
(*George Washington* is a proper noun.)

▶ **Identify and capitalize each proper noun that names a historical period, event, and/or document in the following sentences. Circle all common nouns.**

1. The american revolutionary war lasted from 1775 until 1783.

   _____

2. The boston tea party was an event that led up to the american revolutionary war.

   _____

3. The constitution of the united states begins, "We the people."

   _____

4. The declaration of independence is one of the most important documents in our country.

   _____

5. The battle of gettysburg was one of the major battles of the civil war.

   _____

▶ **Revisit a piece of your writing. Edit the draft to make sure proper nouns are capitalized correctly.**

Capitalizing Titles

> Titles of books, stories, and essays are proper nouns.
> Each important word in a title should begin with a
> capital letter.
>
> Maniac Magee is one of my favorite books.
> (*Maniac Magee* is a book title and a proper noun.)

▶ **Identify the title and which words to capitalize.**

1. My brother wrote an essay called my favorite character. _____

2. Many children have heard a song about rudolph the red-nosed
   reindeer. _____

3. Nora wrote a haiku called the autumn leaves. _____

4. I called my story the bear who slept too late. _____

5. The three little pigs is a classic story. _____

▶ **Revisit a piece of your writing. Edit the draft to make sure proper nouns are
written correctly.**

Capitalizing Languages, People's Names, and Nationalities

> Languages, people's names, races, and nationalities are proper nouns. They should always be capitalized.
>
> She is British. (*British* is a proper noun.)
>
> My daughter speaks French. (*French* is a proper noun)

> **Identify the languages, names, races, and nationalities to capitalize.**

1. My best friend speaks chinese and english. _____

2. harry potter is one of my favorite characters. _____

3. She is native american. _____

4. I was born speaking spanish. _____

5. My clarinet teacher is martin sherman. _____

> **Revisit a piece of your writing. Edit the draft to make sure proper nouns are written correctly.**

Review Proper Nouns

A **proper noun** is a word that names a particular person, place, or thing, and begins with a capital letter.

<u>Shawn</u> works well with others. (*Shawn* is a proper noun)

<u>Six Flags</u> is great amusement park! (*Six Flags* is a proper noun)

▶ **Identify and capitalize the proper nouns in the sentences below.**

1. When she got to school, juliette turned in her homework. _____

2. henry got a new bat for his birthday. _____

3. emily and ken played four square at recess. _____

4. We traveled to chicago over break. _____

5. jackson street market is my favorite place to shop for groceries. _____

▶ **Revisit a piece of your writing. Edit the draft to make sure proper nouns are written correctly.**

Connect to Writing: Using Proper Nouns

▶ **Read the selection and choose the best answer to each question.**
Read the following paragraph about going on vacation. Look for any revisions that should be made. Then answer the questions that follow.

(1) On friday, we are driving to New York City. (2) My Uncle Sam is coming with us. (3) My brother, Joseph wants to see the statue of liberty (4) We are all very excited! (5) I hope we all have a great time!

1. What change should be made in sentence 1?

   A. Sentence 1 should end with a question mark.

   B. In sentence 1, *Friday* should be capitalized.

   C. Make no changes.

   D. Sentence 1 should not have any capitalized words.

2. What change should be made in sentence 3?

   A. It should written with a question mark.

   B. Make no change.

   C. In sentence 3, Statue of Liberty should be capitalized.

   D. Change "wants" to "wanted."

▶ **Write about a city, state, or country you would like to visit someday. Be sure to include proper nouns when necessary.**

_____

_____

_____

_____

Singular Possessive Nouns

> A **singular possessive** noun shows ownership of an object by one person or thing.
> Adding an *apostrophe* and an *s* to a singular noun makes it possessive.
>
> The **dog's** tail is wagging. (*dog's* is the singular possessive noun)
> The **student's** homework is finished. (*student's* is the singular possessive noun)

▷ **Identify the singular possessive noun and write it correctly with an apostrophe on the line after the sentence.**

1. My friends grandpa is a famous artist. _____

2. The chairs fabric is worn. _____

3. My moms favorite food is tomato soup. _____

4. We went to the game and saw the star players trophy. _____

5. The suns rays are bright. _____

6. The houses roof is in need of repair. _____

7. The sandwichs ingredients include turkey, lettuce, and cheese. _____

8. The restaurants best dish is apple pie. _____

9. The horses stall is right next to the tack room. _____

10. The childs mother is standing in line. _____

▷ **Revisit a piece of your writing. Edit the draft to make sure possessive nouns are written correctly.**

Plural Possessive Nouns

> A **plural possessive** noun shows ownership by more than one person or thing.
>
> When a plural noun ends with -*s*, adding an apostrophe makes it possessive. However, for plural nouns that do not end in -*s*, such as men and children, add -'*s* to make the word possessive.
>
> The **children's** schoolbooks were lost. (*children's* is the plural possessive noun)
> The **dresses**' patterns were beautiful. (*dresses*' is the plural possessive noun)

▶ **Identify the plural possessive noun and place the apostrophe correctly in each sentence below.**

1. The football players uniforms were dirty after the game. _____

2. The womens basketball team played well. _____

3. The cooks kitchens were a mess. _____

4. The mens bathroom is located down the hall. _____

5. The students computers are new. _____

▶ **Revisit a piece of your writing. Edit the draft to make sure possessive nouns are written correctly.**

Apostrophe Use in Possessive Nouns

A **singular possessive** noun shows ownership of an object by one person or thing. Adding an apostrophe and an *s* to a singular noun makes it possessive.

A **plural possessive** noun shows ownership by more than one person or thing.
When a plural noun ends with -*s*, adding an apostrophe makes it possessive. However, for plural nouns that do not end in -*s*, such as men and children, add -'*s* to make the word possessive.

▶ **In the phrases below, identify the possessive nouns as singular or plural and correctly place the apostrophe in each word.**

1. queens crowns _____

2. carrots tops _____

3. neighbors yard _____

4. mens suits _____

5. sisters sweater _____

6. pencils erasers _____

7. plants container _____

8. bears den _____

9. kitchens oven _____

10. houses mailboxes _____

▶ **Revisit a piece of your writing. Edit the draft to make sure apostrophes with possessive nouns are written correctly.**

Review Possessive Nouns

A **singular possessive** noun shows ownership of an object by one person or thing. Adding an apostrophe and an s to a singular noun makes it possessive.

A **plural possessive** noun shows ownership by more than one person or thing.
When a plural noun ends with -s, adding an apostrophe makes it possessive. However, for plural nouns that do not end in -s, such as men and children, add -'s to make the word possessive.

▶ **Rewrite the possessive nouns that are in parentheses below, and correctly place the apostrophe in each word.**

1. The (students) assignments were turned in yesterday. _____

2. Her (brothers) guitar is brand new. _____

3. We will find the (problems) solutions. _____

4. We could hear many (dogs) barks last night. _____

5. The (letters) stamps were peeling off the envelopes. _____

6. This (months) water bill is due in one week. _____

7. (Bobs) car window needs to be fixed. _____

8. All the (windows) glass was broken from the storm. _____

9. The (witnesss) testimony helped put the criminal in jail. _____

10. The computers keyboard was damaged. _____

▶ **Revisit a piece of your writing. Edit the draft to make sure possessive nouns are written correctly.**

Connect to Writing: Using Possessive Nouns

▶ **Read the selection and choose the best answer to each question.**

Read the following paragraph about being at school. Look for any revisions that should be made. Then answer the questions that follow.

(1) On Monday, Sarahs project was due. (2) She had to present her project to the class. (3) Marks project was not done. (4) He had to stay in at lunch to finish his project.

1. What change should be made in sentence 1?

    A. "Sarahs" should have an apostrophe *s – Sarah's.*

    B. Sentence 1 should end with a question mark.

    C. Sentence 1 should end with an exclamation point.

    D. Make no changes.

2. What change should be made in sentence 3?

    A. The sentence should be written with a question mark.

    B. "Marks" should have an apostrophe *s – Mark's.*

    C. Sentence 3 should end with an exclamation point.

    D. Make no changes.

▶ **Write about an important project or presentation you gave in school. Be sure to include proper punctuation when using possessive nouns.**

_____

_____

_____

_____

Subject and Object Pronouns

A **pronoun** is a word that takes the place of a noun such as, *he*, *she*, or *they*.
A **subject pronoun** tells who or what does the action of a sentence. An **object pronoun** tells who or what receives the action of the verb.

He skied down the mountain. (*He* is the subject)
John watched him. (*him* is the object)

▶ **Identify whether the underlined pronoun in each sentence is a subject pronoun or an object pronoun.**

1. Uncle Mike watched her after school. _____

2. He came to school early to meet with his teacher. _____

3. She cares for horses on the weekend. _____

4. Jodi brought the present to her. _____

5. They cheered on the home team. _____

▶ **Revisit a piece of your writing. Edit the draft to make sure subject and object pronouns are written correctly.**

Reflexive and Demonstrative Pronouns

A **reflexive pronoun** is a pronoun whose antecedent is the subject of the sentence and ends in –*self* or -*selves*. A **demonstrative pronoun** is used to point out particular people or things. *This* is used to talk about one person or thing that is nearby; *these* is used to talk about more than one person or thing nearby. *That* is used to talk about one thing far away; *those* is used to talk about more than one person or thing far away.

> The pitcher injured <u>herself</u> when she slipped on the mound. (Reflexive)
> <u>These</u> players will take over pitching for the rest of the game. (Demonstrative)

▸ **Identify whether the underlined pronoun in each sentence below is reflexive or demonstrative.**

1. Ben made dinner by <u>himself</u>. _____

2. <u>These</u> look beautiful. _____

3. I will never forget <u>this</u>. _____

4. I wrote the paper by <u>myself</u>. _____

5. They went to the pizza place by <u>themselves</u>. _____

▸ **Revisit a piece of your writing. Edit the draft to make sure subject and object pronouns are written correctly.**

Pronoun-Antecedent Agreement

A **pronoun** is a word, such as *he*, *she*, or *they*, that takes the place of one or more nouns.

An **antecedent** is the word or phrase a pronoun replaces. The antecedent may be in the same sentence, or it may fall in a previous sentence.

When an antecedent is singular, the pronoun that replaces it must also be singular. When an antecedent is plural, the pronoun that replaces it must be plural, too.

> *Hank* wants to be a scientist, so he studies hard in his science classes. (*Hank* is the singular antecedent; *he* is the singular pronoun.)
> *Hank* and *Sandy* have an earth science test tomorrow. They will study this afternoon. (*Hank* and *Sally* is the plural antecedent; *they* is the plural pronoun.)

▶ **Identify the pronoun and antecedent in the following sentences.**

1. Bill delivered his speech to the class even though he was nervous.

_____

2. Emily called her friend.

_____

3. Clark and Sherman finished their homework before class was over.

_____

4. Jack went to see his grandparents.

_____

5. Beth and Joey went to their jobs early.

_____

▶ **Revisit a piece of your writing. Edit the draft to make sure subject and object pronouns are written correctly.**

Review Pronouns

A **subject pronoun** tells who or what does the action of a sentence. An **object pronoun** tells who or what receives the action of the verb.

A **reflexive pronoun** is a pronoun whose antecedent is the subject of the sentence and ends in -*self* or -*selves*.

A **demonstrative pronoun** is used to point out particular people or things.

> Identify each underlined pronoun below as subject, object, reflexive, or demonstrative in each of the sentences below.

1. Kristen typed <u>her</u> paper on the computer. _____

2. James sang on the stage by <u>himself</u>. _____

3. Sandy and Tammy worked hard to help <u>her</u>. _____

4. I love <u>those</u>! _____

5. Mark and Marsha gave <u>their</u> mom a birthday present. _____

> Revisit a piece of your writing. Edit the draft to make sure pronouns are used correctly.

Connect to Writing: Using Pronouns

> **Read the selection and choose the best answer to each question.**

Read the following paragraph about going to a movie with a friend. Look for any revisions that should be made. Then answer the questions that follow.

(1) On Saturday night, Kelly and I saw a movie. (2) Kelly and I saw the movie *Finding Nemo*. (3) The movie theater wasn't busy and we got good seats. (4) Kelly had popcorn and Kelly had soda. (5) I had popcorn and chocolate.

1. How can you combine sentences 1 and 2 using pronouns when appropriate?

   A. The sentences should not be combined.

   B. On Saturday night, Kelly and I saw a movie, Kelly and I saw the movie *Finding Nemo*.

   C. On Saturday night, Kelly and I saw the movie *Finding Nemo*.

   D. On Saturday night, Kelly and I saw a movie, it was *Finding Nemo*.

2. What changes can you make to sentence 4?

   A. Kelly had popcorn, Kelly had soda, I had popcorn and chocolate.

   B. Kelly had popcorn and she also had soda.

   C. Make no changes.

   D. Kelly had popcorn.

> **Write about a movie you've seen and the experience you had. Be sure to include pronouns, when necessary, to help make your writing more smooth for the reader.**

_____

_____

_____

_____

Possessive Pronouns with Nouns and Alone

A **possessive pronoun** is a pronoun that shows ownership, such as *your*, *her*, *his*, *our*, and *their*.

> That new <u>bike</u> is his. (*his* is a possessive pronoun)
>
> That is <u>their</u> new puppy. (*their* is a possessive pronoun)

▶ **Replace the possessive noun in parentheses with the correct possessive pronoun.**

1. Jan and (Jan's) brother met Sam at the park. _____

2. There is a stream behind (Tom's) house. _____

3. (Aaron and Katie's) dog ran away. _____

4. My family wants to spend time with (some) relatives in New York City. _____

5. Is that (belongs to you) puppy? _____

▶ **Revisit a piece of your writing. Edit the draft to make sure possessive pronouns are used correctly.**

Using Possessive Pronouns

A **possessive pronoun** is a pronoun that shows ownership, such as *mine*, *yours*, *his*, *hers*, *ours*, and *theirs*. Some possessive pronouns are used before nouns and others can stand alone.

> That red coat is <u>mine</u>. (*mine* is a possessive pronoun)

> These papers are <u>yours</u>. (*yours* is a possessive pronoun)

> **Underline the possessive pronoun that stands alone in the following sentences.**

1. Those books are yours.
2. The backpack and the pencil box are hers.
3. I forgot mine again.
4. Where did they buy theirs?
5. Which notebook is his?

> **Revisit a piece of your writing. Edit the draft to make sure possessive pronouns are used correctly.**

Using Possessive Pronouns

> A **possessive pronoun** is a pronoun that shows
> ownership, such as *mine, your(s), his, her(s), ours,* and
> *their(s).* Some possessive pronouns are used before
> nouns and others can stand alone.
>
> These are <u>his</u> keys and those are <u>yours</u>.
> (*his* is a possessive pronoun followed by a noun;
> *yours* is a possessive pronoun that stands alone
> and is not followed by a noun.)

▶ **Underline the possessive pronoun that is followed by a noun in the sentences
below. Double underline the possessive pronoun that stands alone and is not
followed by a noun.**

1. Your books are over there, and these are mine.

2. Their house is smaller than yours.

3. Her mom works at the school just like ours.

4. My puzzles are new like theirs.

5. His bicycle is older than hers.

▶ **Revisit a piece of your writing. Edit the draft to make sure possessive pronouns
are used correctly.**

Name _____

Review Possessive Pronouns

A **possessive pronoun** is a pronoun that shows
ownership, such as *mine, your(s), his, her(s), ours,* and
their(s) and can take the place of a possessive noun.
Some possessive pronouns are used before nouns and
others can stand alone.

Sally loves her new puppy. (her)
Those sneakers look exactly like mine. (mine)

▸ **For each word pair, write a sentence that uses the possessive pronoun
correctly.**

1. (presents, yours) _____

2. (his, paintings) _____

3. (shirts, their) _____

4. (house, theirs) _____

5. (tools, ours) _____

▸ **Revisit a piece of your writing. Edit the draft to make sure possessive pronouns
are used correctly.**

Connect to Writing: Using Possessive Pronouns

> Read the selection and choose the best answer to each question.

Read the following paragraph about watching a baseball game. Look for any revisions that should be made. Then answer the questions that follow.

(1) Adam and Adam's brother are playing baseball. (2) They are playing at the park while their mom is working. (3) So, their father is watching them play at the park. (4) Soon they will go home to fix supper.

1. What changes should be made in sentence 1?

    A. Adam and Adam's brother are playing Baseball.

    B. Adam and his brother are playing baseball.

    C. Adam and Adams brother are playing baseball.

    D. Make no changes.

2. What changes should be made in sentence 3?

    A. Adam's father is at the park. Adam's father is watching them play baseball.

    B. So their father is watching them play at the park?

    C. So, they're father is watching them play at the park.

    D. Make no changes.

> Write about a time you played baseball, watched a baseball game, or played in the park. Be sure to include possessive pronouns when necessary.

_____

_____

_____

_____

Using *I* and *Me*

> A **subject pronoun** is a type of pronoun that tells who or what does the action of the sentence. An **object pronoun** is a type of pronoun that tells who or what receives the action of the verb. *I* is used as the subject of a sentence. *Me* is the object.
>
> Liam and I went to the store. (*I* is a subject pronoun.)
>
> Sam played with Kay and **me** at recess. (*Me* is an object pronoun.)

▶ **Fill in the blank with I or me. Make sure to consider whether the pronoun is the subject or the object.**

1. _____ picked up my laundry and put it in the wash.

2. Sam cooked breakfast for Morgan and _____.

3. Ross and _____ worked together on the history project.

4. Will you and mom help _____ clean my room?

5. The teacher helped Jane and _____ with the math assignment.

▶ **Revisit a piece of your writing. Edit the draft to make sure pronouns are used correctly.**

Using the Right Pronoun

A **subject pronoun** is a type of pronoun that tells who or what does the action of the sentence. An **object pronoun** is a type of pronoun that tells who or what receives the action of the verb.

Where are the birds? **They** flew away.

(*They* is the pronoun that replaces the *birds*.)

> Use the correct pronoun in the sentences below.

1. Where is Lance? _____ is at work.

2. The books are on the table. _____ belong to Mary.

3. My family went to the park. _____ were having a party.

4. Where is Mrs. Brown? _____ is in the kitchen.

5. I want to see the tiger. _____ is hiding behind a rock.

> Revisit a piece of your writing. Edit the draft to make sure pronouns are used correctly.

Reflexive Pronouns

> A **reflexive pronoun** is a type of pronoun that tells when the subject of a sentence does something to itself. A reflexive pronoun is used when the subject and object of a sentence are the same person/thing or people/things.
>
> A reflexive pronoun ends in *-self* or *-selves* such as *herself, himself, themselves, ourselves, myself.*
>
> We finished the project by **ourselves**. (*ourselves* is the reflexive pronoun)

▶ **Choose the correct reflexive pronoun for each sentence below.**

1. Maggie went to the store by _____.

2. They wanted to go to the movies by _____.

3. He rode his bike to school by _____.

4. I finished cooking dinner by _____.

5. The statue was in a display case by _____.

▶ **Revisit a piece of your writing. Edit the draft to make sure pronouns are used correctly.**

Review Correct Pronouns

> The pronoun *I* is the subject of a sentence, and the pronoun *me* is used after action verbs and after prepositions such as *to*, *with*, *for*, or *at*. Always name yourself last when talking about yourself and another person.
>
> **Reflexive pronouns** are used when the subject and object of a sentence are the same person/thing or people/things.

> ▶ **Use the correct pronoun in each sentence below.**

1. Abby and _____ walk the dogs after school.

2. We went to the store by _____.

3. John bought sandwiches for Luis and _____.

4. I went to the play by _____.

5. Will Hector be able to come with Anatoli and _____?

> ▶ **Revisit a piece of your writing. Edit the draft to make sure pronouns are used correctly.**

Connect to Writing: Using the Correct Pronoun

> Read the selection and choose the best answer to each question.

Read the following paragraph about how some friends spent their Saturday together. Look for any revisions that should be made. Then answer the questions that follow.

(1) Dana and Corbin went to get ice cream. (2) Dana and Corbin both like chocolate ice cream. (3) Dana and Corbin both got chocolate shakes. (4) After they had ice cream, they went to the park. (5) While at the park, Dana and Corbin sat by the fountain.

1. How can you combine sentences 1 and 2 using pronouns to make it sound more smooth?

   A. Dana and Corbin went to get ice cream and like chocolate.

   B. Make no changes.

   C. Dana and Corbin went to get ice cream and they both like chocolate.

   D. You cannot combine sentences 1 and 2.

2. What changes should be made in sentence 3?

   A. End the sentence with a question mark.

   B. Make no changes.

   C. Combine sentences 3 and 4.

   D. Do not capitalize "Dana" or "Corbin."

> Write about a time you spent with a friend over the weekend. Be sure to use correct pronouns in your writing.

_____

_____

_____

_____

Pronoun Contractions

A **pronoun** is a word that takes the place of a noun.
A **contraction** is a short way of writing two words,
using an apostrophe to replace one or more letters.
Some pronouns can be combined with some verbs to
form contractions.

I am excited to see the concert!
I'm excited to see the concert!

▷ **Change the pronoun and verb into a contraction in the sentences below.**

1. I am ready for spring break. _____

2. We are very glad that the game is tonight. _____

3. You are my best friend. _____

4. I know they are going to ride bikes to school. _____

5. It is still snowing outside. _____

▷ **Revisit a piece of your writing. Edit the draft to make sure pronoun contractions are used correctly.**

Pronouns and Homophones

A **contraction** is a short way of writing two words, using an apostrophe to replace one or more letters. Some pronouns can be combined with some verbs to form contractions.

Homophones are words that sound the same but have different meanings and spellings. Some pronoun contractions are homophones.

It's time to get up for school.
The cat drank its milk quickly.

> **Underline the correct homophone in each sentence below.**

1. Their/They're going to run laps on the track.

2. I know it's/its going to be a long winter.

3. You're/Your new coat is nice.

4. Their/They're car is parked in the parking lot.

5. The dog likes to chase it's/its tail.

> **Revisit a piece of your writing. Edit the draft to make sure pronouns and homophones are used correctly.**

Review Pronouns and Homophones

A **pronoun** is a word that takes the place of a noun.
A **contraction** is a short way of writing two words,
using an apostrophe to replace one or more letters.
Some pronouns can be combined with some verbs to
form contractions.

> She's making breakfast. (*She* is the pronoun. *She*
> and *is* are combined to make the contraction.)

▶ **Identify the pronoun and the pronoun/verb combination that make the
contraction in the sentences below.**

1. They've finished practicing for the spelling bee. _____

2. Did you know that you're taller than my brother is? _____

3. I know she'll be on time for the play. _____

4. He's going shopping with his friend. _____

5. You're going to Grandma's house this weekend. _____

▶ **Revisit a piece of your writing. Edit the draft to make sure pronoun
contractions are used correctly.**

Review Pronoun Contractions

Pronouns can be combined with some verbs to form contractions, and you can use an apostrophe (') to take the place of the letter or letters they leave out to form the contraction.

We'll go as soon as the taxicab arrives.
They've already finished cleaning out the car.

▶ **Write the correct contraction from the pronoun and verb combination in each sentence below.**

1. I know she is coming early to the meeting. _____

2. You are going to be late if you don't hurry. _____

3. He is taking an art class over the summer. _____

4. They are planning a trip to California. _____

5. We will get to sit in the front row at the concert. _____

▶ **Revisit a piece of your writing. Edit the draft to make sure pronoun contractions are used correctly.**

Connect to Writing: Using Pronoun Contractions

> **Read the selection and choose the best answer to each question.**

Read the following paragraph about a day at the beach. Look for any revisions that should be made. Then answer the questions that follow.

(1) The whole family is meeting at the beach today. (2) We're going to have lunch and play games. (3) Their all bringing a dish to share. (4) I told my cousin, "I know your excited!" (5) We made sand castles, swam, and had a great meal! (6) We're going to plan another trip later this month. (7) I can't wait!

1. What changes can be made to sentence 3?

   A. They're all bringing a dish to share.

   B. End the sentence with a question mark.

   C. They are all bringing a dish to share!

   D. Make no changes.

2. What changes can be made to sentence 4?

   A. Remove the comma in the sentence.

   B. I told my cousin, "I know you're excited!"

   C. Remove the quotation marks in the sentence.

   D. Make no changes.

> **Write about a special time you had with your family. Be sure to use correct pronoun contractions in your writing.**

_____

_____

_____

_____

Action Verbs

> A **verb** is a word that shows action.
>
> An **action verb** is a word that tells what a person or thing does.
>
>   Sammy <u>climbed</u> the tree. (action verb)

▶ **Underline the *action verb* in each sentence.**

1. Students rush to class.

2. Police catch criminals.

3. He called his friend on the phone.

4. He worked on Saturday and Sunday.

5. The airplane landed safely.

6. The team practiced after school.

7. She turned up the music.

8. The students ate lunch.

9. They quit the game early.

10. The horses ran in the fields.

▶ **Revisit a piece of your writing. Edit the draft to make sure all action verbs are used correctly.**

Main Verbs and Helping Verbs

A **verb** is a word that shows action. Some verbs are more than one word. The **main verb** is the most important verb. The **helping verb** comes before the main verb and tells more about the action. Helping verbs include *is, are, has, have, had, should, would, could, can,* and *may*.

The birds <u>are flying</u> south for the winter. (*are* – helping verb; *flying* – main verb)

> Circle the *main verb* in each sentence. Underline the *helping verb*.

1. The fish are swimming in the pond.

2. The tree should grow several feet this year.

3. He is paddling the boat.

4. They may study for hours.

5. The bus is carrying many passengers.

6. The car can carry five passengers.

7. You should watch when crossing the street.

8. The team is playing the last home game of the year.

9. They are riding their bikes to school.

10. The bread is baking in the oven.

> Revisit a piece of your writing. Edit the draft to make sure all main and helping verbs are used correctly.

Linking Verbs

A **linking verb** tells what someone or something is or is like. Most linking verbs are forms of the verb *be*, such as *is*, *are*, and *were*. However, other words can be linking verbs, too. These words include *appear*, *become*, and *seem*.

The children <u>are</u> excited to ride the train. (linking verb)

> Underline the *linking verb* in each sentence.

1. The thunderstorm is approaching.

2. He was walking home after school.

3. They were practicing before the concert.

4. I was happy about my test score.

5. She appeared pale after lunch.

6. They are cooking dinner together.

7. Kevin's shoes are muddy.

8. The old house was spooky.

9. The dogs in the park were playful.

10. Summer seemed shorter this year.

> **Revisit a piece of your writing. Edit the draft to make sure all linking verbs are used correctly.**

Review Verbs

> A **verb** shows action.
> An **action verb** tells what a person or thing does.
> Some verbs are more than one word. The **main verb** is the most important verb.
> The **helping verb** comes before the main verb.
> A **linking verb** tells what someone or something is or is like. Most linking verbs
> are forms of the verb *be*. The words *appear*, *become*, and *seem* can also be
> linking verbs.

▶ Underline the *linking verb/main verb* or *helping verb/main verb* combination in each sentence.

1. They should make the park free to enter.

2. The cookies appear done.

3. They are growing vegetables in the garden.

4. We should make peace with our friends.

5. The contestants seem nervous to play the game.

6. The children seem ready for recess.

7. The teacher was grateful for the gifts she received from her class.

8. All of the dishes are spotless.

9. The enemy has decided to surrender.

10. The track team is performing well.

▶ Revisit a piece of your writing. Edit the draft to make sure all verbs are used correctly.

Connect to Writing: Using Action, Main, Helping, and Linking Verbs

> Read the selection and choose the best answer to each question.

Read the following paragraph about watching your favorite band play live on stage. Look for any revisions that should be made. Then answer the questions that follow.

(1) We are going to see our favorite band play tonight. (2) My friends and I are very excited to see the band play live in the park. (3) The band might play our favorite songs. (4) It was such a great day for the show. (5) We met many great people today. (6) We have enjoyed listening to the band and meeting new friends!

1. Identify the main and helping verbs in sentence 3.

   A. favorite, songs
   B. The, band
   C. might, play
   D. There are no main or helping verbs in the sentence.

2. Identify the main and helping verbs in sentence 6.

   A. We, have
   B. have, enjoyed
   C. enjoyed, listening
   D. There are no main or helping verbs in the sentence.

> Write about a special event you spent with family or friends. Be sure to use verbs in your writing correctly.

_____

_____

_____

Name _____

Past, Present, and Future Tenses

A verb in the **present tense** shows action that is happening now.

A verb in the **past tense** shows action that has already happened.

A verb in the **future tense** shows action that will happen.

> He <u>sings</u> on stage. (present tense)
>
> He <u>sang</u> on stage. (past tense)
>
> He <u>will sing</u> on stage. (future tense)

▶ **Underline the *verb* in each sentence, and tell when the action happens.**

1. Juan likes going to the movies. _____

2. We loved his last film. _____

3. I watched the film last weekend. _____

4. April will meet us at the game. _____

5. The audience loved the show. _____

6. Grandpa arrived early to the appointment. _____

7. We will see the band play tomorrow night. _____

8. She knows she is ready for the test. _____

9. I go to the library once a week. _____

10. They will travel to Springfield next week. _____

▶ **Revisit a piece of your writing. Edit the draft to make sure all verb tenses are used correctly.**

Helping Verbs and Past Participles

The past tense of a regular verb is formed by adding
-ed to its present form. When used with a helping verb,
such as *has*, *have*, or *had*, it is called the **past participle.**

The singer <u>has memorized</u> the song. (*has* –
helping verb; *memorized* – past participle)

> Underline the *helping verb* and *past participle* in each sentence.

1. The class has earned a reward.

2. They have performed many shows.

3. I have worked on the school newspaper.

4. Jan had developed a new scoring system.

5. He has visited here before.

6. Stephanie and Richard have seen the band play.

7. They have eaten at that restaurant before.

8. We have wanted to buy a new car.

9. He has talked to his teacher about the test.

10. The bird had left its nest.

> **Revisit a piece of your writing. Edit the draft to make sure all verb tenses are used correctly.**

Consistent Use of Tenses

When sentences tell about events in one particular time, all the verbs should be in the same tense. Use all present tense verbs to talk or write about actions in the present. Use all past tense verbs to talk or write about the past. Use all future tense verbs to talk or write about the future.

> Sonny <u>will meet</u> me at the park. (*will meet,* future)
> Ann <u>stayed</u> at her friend's house last weekend. (*stayed,* past)

> **Rewrite each sentence to match the tense shown in parentheses.**

1. Ryan took his test on Monday. (future)

_____

2. Emily will talk about Martin Luther King, Jr. during her speech. (past)

_____

3. She ate her lunch at the table. (present)

_____

> **Complete each sentence with *has* or *have*.**

4. We _____ played this game before.

5. Shawna _____ decided to walk to work.

6. My mom and dad _____ gone to see the play.

7. The farmer _____ harvested this year's crop.

> **Revisit a piece of your writing. Edit the draft to make sure all verb tenses are used correctly.**

_____

Review Verb Tenses

A verb in the **present tense** shows action that is happening now.

A verb in the **past tense** shows action that has already happened.

A verb in the **future tense** shows action that will happen.

Jim <u>will start</u> preschool next year. (*will start*, future)

Laci <u>attends</u> preschool this year. (*attends*, present)

Conner <u>finished</u> preschool last year. (*finished*, past)

▶ **Change the following sentences from the present tense to both *past* and *future* tenses.**

1. Martin gives his speech.

_____

2. He sharpens his pencil.

_____

3. She cooks dinner.

_____

4. Mom washes the car.

_____

5. The students finish their homework.

_____

▶ **Revisit a piece of your writing. Edit the draft to make sure all verb tenses are used correctly.**

Connect to Writing: Using Verb Tenses Correctly

▶ **Read the selection and choose the best answer to each question.**

Read the following paragraph about watching a singer on stage. Look for any revisions that should be made. Then answer the questions that follow.

> (1) The singer wears a special outfit on stage. (2) He sang their favorite songs. (3) The audience danced to the music. (4) Everyone sang along. (5) The band played late into the night.

1. What is the correct past tense version of sentence 1?

   A. The singer weared a special outfit on stage.

   B. The singer wear a special outfit on stage.

   C. The singer wore a special outfit on stage.

   D. The singer wores a special outfit on stage.

2. What is the correct present tense version of sentence 3?

   A. The audience dances to the music.

   B. The audience dance to the music.

   C. The audience will dance to the music.

   D. The sentence is written in the present tense.

▶ **Write about a favorite time you had with friends and family. Be sure to use correct verb tenses throughout your writing.**

_____

_____

_____

_____

Present Progressive Verb Tense

The **progressive verb tense** tells about action that happens over a period of time.

The **present progressive verb tense** tells about action that is happening in the present.

It is formed by using the present tense form of *be* (*am/is/are*) and adding *-ing* to the present tense form of the verb.

> Maggie is <u>traveling</u> to California by train.
> (-ing added to travel)

> **Write the present progressive verb in each sentence, and tell what is the present tense of the verb *be*.**

1. The bus is arriving in Chicago. _____

2. Many bands are marching in the parade. _____

3. I am getting excited about the concert! _____

4. Ben and Scott are walking around the track. _____

5. Annie is barking at the mail carrier. _____

> **Revisit a piece of your writing. Edit the draft to make sure all present progressive verb tenses are used correctly.**

Past Progressive Verb Tense

The **progressive verb tense** tells about action that happens over a period of time.

The **past progressive verb tense** tells about action that happened over a period of time in the past but is no longer taking place.

The past progressive is formed by using the past tense form of *be* (*was/were*) and adding *-ing* to the present tense verb.

> Yesterday, I was working on my project.
> Last year, we were learning how to play the piano.

> ▶ **Identify the past progressive verb in each sentence and the past tense form of the verb *be*.**

1. Kate and Jess were eating lunch. _____

2. The wind was blowing gently. _____

3. Aunt Ida was writing a letter. _____

4. Gabe was running in the gym. _____

5. Mr. Johnson and Mr. Smith were ordering food for the team. _____
_____

> ▶ **Revisit a piece of your writing. Edit the draft to make sure all past progressive verb tenses are used correctly.**

Name _____

Future Progressive Verb Tense

The **progressive verb tense** tells about action that happens over a period of time.

The **future progressive verb tense** tells about action that will happen over a period of time in the future. It is formed by using *will be* and adding *-ing* to the verb.

   I <u>will be working</u> on this project for weeks.
   I <u>will be attending</u> the wedding with my family.

▶ **Identify the future progressive verb tense in the following sentences.**

1. Jenna and Brianna will be thinking of a new game. _____

2. Jimmy and Tony will be riding the train. _____

3. We will be going to the museum in March. _____

4. They will be driving to her house. _____

5. She will be ordering pizza. _____

▶ **Revisit a piece of your writing. Edit the draft to make sure all future progressive verb tenses are used correctly.**

Review Progressive Verb Tenses

The **present progressive verb tense** tells about action that is happening in the present.
It is formed by using the present tense form of *be* and adding *-ing* to the verb.

The **past progressive verb tense** tells about action that happened over a period of time in the past. It is formed by using the past tense form of *be* and adding *-ing* to the verb.

The **future progressive verb tense** tells about action that will happen over a period of time in the future. It is formed by using *will be* and adding *-ing* to the verb.

▷ **Identify the verb phrase in each sentence and tell if it is present, past, or future progressive tense.**

1. Spencer and Gus are running late for work. _____

2. Dora was babysitting on Saturday. _____

3. They will be riding in the van with us. _____

4. They are opening the school doors. _____

5. Everyone will be riding the roller coaster. _____

▷ **Revisit a piece of your writing. Edit the draft to make sure all progressive verb tenses are used correctly.**

Connect to Writing: Using Progressive Verb Tenses

> **Read the selection and choose the best answer to each question.**

Read the following paragraph about making cookies with friends. Look for any revisions that should be made. Then answer the questions that follow

(1) My friends are coming over to my house. (2) They walk over around 2 o'clock. (3) We baked cookies. (4) Everyone will taste them. (5) Then they will walk home when we are finished. (6) Everyone will take some cookies with them.

1. Using the progressive verb tense, what changes can be made to sentence 2?

   A. They are walking over around 2 o'clock.

   B. They walked over around 2 o'clock.

   C. They did walk over around 2 o'clock.

   D. Make no changes.

2. Using the progressive verb tense, what changes can be made to sentence 3?

   A. We bake cookies.

   B. We are baking cookies.

   C. We has baked cookies.

   D. Make no changes.

> **Write about a time you cooked with your friends or family. Write about the experiences that you had using the progressive verb tense.**

_____

_____

_____

_____

May, Might, Can, and *Could*

A **modal auxiliary** is a helping verb that shows how things could be or should be. Some tell how likely or unlikely it is that an action will happen.

may, might—the action could take place but is not likely
can—it is possible that the action will take place
could—likelihood is unknown or unlikely that something may happen

> Julie **might go** to the party. (could take place)
> Allison **could feel** better by then. (likelihood unknown)

▶ **Indicate the modal auxiliary in each sentence and identify whether it means that the situation *could take place, is possible,* or *likelihood unknown*.**

1. Lana might go on the field trip. _____

2. Norah can play the piano after she is done with her homework.

_____

3. Jared could drive us to the game. _____

4. Dr. Smart may attend the workshop. _____

5. She can finish reading the book by noon. _____

▶ **Revisit a piece of your writing. Edit the draft to make sure all modal auxiliaries with *may, might, can*, and *could* are used correctly.**

Would, Should, and Must

A **modal auxiliary** is a helping verb that shows how things could be or should be. Some modal auxiliaries express the feelings or opinion of the writer or speaker.

would—the writer expresses <u>willingness</u>
should—the writer is <u>suggesting</u> an action
must—the writer expresses a <u>need</u> for something to happen

> He **must learn** more about the plot of the story. (need)
> I **should finish** my homework before I play outside. (suggestion)

▶ **Identify the modal auxiliary in each sentence and tell whether the sentence expresses a *suggestion*, a *willingness*, or a *need*.**

1. Abdul should go home. _____

2. He must pass the math test to get a passing grade. _____

3. Shelly would go if she had a note from her mother. _____

4. Joey should walk with his little sister. _____

5. Michael and Damon must see the teacher before recess. _____

▶ **Revisit a piece of your writing. Edit the draft to make sure all modal auxiliaries using *would*, *should*, and *must* are used correctly.**

Using Modal Auxiliaries

A **modal auxiliary** is a helping verb that shows how things could be or should be. Some modal auxiliaries express the feelings or opinion of the writer or speaker. Modal auxiliaries help writers state their ideas clearly. Often, you can change the meaning of a sentence by changing the modal auxiliary.

If it snows, you **might** not have school. (could take place)
You **must** wear a hat and gloves. (expresses a need)

▶ **To complete each sentence, choose a modal auxiliary that expresses your idea or opinion. Write it on the line. Also, write its meaning on the line. Choose from the following phrases to describe the meaning of the modal auxiliary you use: could take place, but is not likely; possible; likelihood unknown; willingness; suggestion; need.**

1. If you travel to Chicago, you _____ go to the art museum.

_____

2. It _____ rain tonight.

_____

3. Ben and Brady _____ have cupcakes for snack.

_____

4. Danny _____ read to his younger brother.

_____

5. Donna _____ miss the opening of the show if she is late.

_____

▶ **Revisit a piece of your writing. Edit the draft to make sure all modal auxiliaries are used correctly.**

Review Modal Auxiliaries

A **modal auxiliary** is a helping verb that shows how things could be or should be. Some tell how likely or unlikely it is that an action will happen.

- **may, might**—the action could take place but is not likely
- **can**—it is possible that the action will take place
- **could**—it is unknown how likely or unlikely that something may happen

Some modal auxiliaries express the feelings or opinion of the writer or speaker.
- **would**—the writer expresses willingness
- **should**—the writer is suggesting an action
- **must**—the writer expresses a need for something to happen

▶ **Identify the modal auxiliaries in the following sentences and explain the meaning of each one.**

1. I think she should read the book to herself. _____

2. He might want to go see the nurse if he's not feeling well. _____

3. You must try the new yogurt shop. _____

4. Eden might read ahead in her new book. _____

5. Justin can always play the game tomorrow. _____

▶ **Revisit a piece of your writing. Edit the draft to make sure all modal auxiliaries are used correctly.**

Connect to Writing: Using Modal Auxiliaries

> **Read the selection and choose the best answer to each question.**

Read the following paragraph about a classroom movie reward. Look for any revisions that should be made. Then answer the questions that follow.

(1) The students have earned a reward movie party for finishing their novels. (2) They must have finished all of their work before watching the movie. (3) The teacher thinks the students might like the movie better than the book. (4) After they watch the movie, the students think they should compare the movie and the book.

1. What is the meaning of the modal auxiliary used in sentence 2?

   A. must, suggestion

   B. must, could take place

   C. must, need

   D. There is no modal auxiliary used in the sentence.

2. What is the meaning of the modal auxiliary used in sentence 4?

   A. should, suggestion

   B. should, could take place

   C. should, need

   D. There is no modal auxiliary used in the sentence

> **Write about a time your class earned a special reward or about a special reward you would like to earn in your classroom. Be sure to use modal auxiliaries in your writing.**

_____

_____

_____

_____

Irregular Verbs

An **irregular verb** is a verb that does not end in *-ed* in the past tense. The spelling of irregular verbs must be memorized.

I **thought** he was going to pick me up after school.
My sister **brought** me a book about California.

▶ **Write the correct form of the verb in parentheses to show *past action*.**

1. The baseball _____ the car window. (strike)

2. She _____ the test yesterday. (take)

3. The players _____ each other high fives. (give)

4. The plot of the story _____ as a shock. (come)

5. They _____ paper airplanes outside. (fly)

6. He _____ a funny story at breakfast. (tell)

7. The students _____ up balloons. (blow)

8. The cook _____ the eggs into a bowl. (break)

9. As soon as he dropped his line in the lake, my dad _____ a fish! (catch)

10. After dinner, Sanjay _____ the cat. (feed)

▶ **Revisit a piece of your writing. Edit the draft to make sure all irregular verbs are used correctly.**

The Verb *Be*

> The special verb *be* does not show action. It tells what
> someone or something is or is like. The verb *be* has
> special forms for different tenses and different subjects.
>
> The weather (is, are) changing. *is*
> Rain (was, were) falling all day. *was*

> **Choose the correct version of the verb *be* to complete each sentence.**

1. Snow (is, are) piling up on the ground outside. _____

2. The sun (was, were) shining brightly this morning. _____

3. The band (is, are) playing very loudly. _____

4. We (was, were) planning to see a movie. _____

5. There (were, will be) a test later this week. _____

6. There (was, were) many clouds in the sky this morning. _____

7. My mother (is, are) a fire fighter. _____

8. Randall (was, were) born in 2010. _____

9. She (is, will be) 11 years old on her next birthday. _____

10. Malia and Mikayla (was, were) in a play last year. _____

> **Revisit a piece of your writing. Edit the draft to make sure the verb *be* is used
correctly.**

Helping Verbs

An **irregular verb** is a verb that does not end in -*ed* in the past tense. Most irregular verbs change spelling when they are used with helping verbs. Often the new spelling uses an *n* or *en* to show past tense.
Helping verbs are verbs that come before a verb, such as *had*, *have*, and *have*.

> Mr. Egler (has taken, has took) several trips to the museum. (*has taken*)

> **Underline the correct helping verbs in each sentence below.**

1. The twins (have grown, have grew) several inches since I saw them last.

2. The doctor (has written, has wrote) many prescriptions this month.

3. The class (had taken, had took) the same test last week.

4. No one (has done, had did) more work on the project than Kate.

5. Each student (has chose, has chosen) a book to read.

6. The baby birds (have flown, have flyed) away from the nest.

7. All the leaves on the tree (has fallen, have fallen).

8. The truck driver (has driven, have driven) in 38 different states.

9. The pond (has frozen, had frozen), so we can go ice skating!

10. The dog (has hided, has hidden) bones all over the yard.

> **Revisit a piece of your writing. Edit the draft to make sure all helping verbs are used correctly.**

Review Irregular Verbs

Verbs that do not add -ed to show past action are called **irregular verbs**. The spellings of irregular verbs must be memorized.

The special verb **be** does not show action. It tells what someone or something is or is like. The verb *be* has special forms for different tenses and different subjects.

> I **bought** a game with my birthday money.
> Juniper **is** my cousin.

> Identify the correct verb in each sentence and name the verb tense.

1. She (make, made) up a funny story during recess. _____

2. The wind (was, were) blowing hard this morning. _____

3. I (am, is) watching my favorite show. _____

4. The puppy (had taken, had took) the toy away from the kitten. _____

5. When Nicki asked if I would go, I (say, said) yes. _____

> Revisit a piece of your writing. Edit the draft to make sure all irregular verbs are used correctly.

Connect to Writing: Using Irregular Verbs

> **Read the selection and choose the best answer to each question.**

Read the following paragraph about making cookies for a family party. Look for any revisions that should be made. Then answer the questions that follow.

(1) My grandmother has a birthday on Saturday. (2) I plan to wore a blue dress to the party. (3) My cousins will all be there. (4) My mom make chocolate chip cookies yesterday to take to the party. (5) They are Grandma's favorite kind. (6) Dad is driving us there.

1. What change should be made to sentence 2?

   A. I plan to wear a blue dress to the party.

   B. I plan to wore a blue dress, to the party.

   C. I planned to wore a blue dress to the party.

   D. Make no change.

2. Which of these sentences from the paragraph is written incorrectly?

   A. My cousins will all be there.

   B. My grandmother has a birthday on Saturday.

   C. My mom make chocolate chip cookies yesterday to take to the party.

   D. They are Grandma's favorite kind.

> **Write a short paragraph about eating cookies or cake with your family or friends. Be sure to include irregular verbs in your writing.**

_____

_____

_____

_____

Present Participles

The **present participle** of regular verbs is formed by adding -*ing* to the verb. If the verb ends in *e*, drop the *e* before adding -*ing*.

    walk + ing = walking
    move + ing = moving

The **participle** form of a verb can be used as an adjective.

    The <u>soaring</u> eagle climbs higher in the sky.

▷ On the line, write the present participle form of the verb shown in parentheses.

1. The (tower) _____ sequoia trees are really a sight to see!

2. The (shift) _____ sunlight shines through the branches and onto the forest floor.

3. We saw several (forage) _____ squirrels on our hike.

4. A (feast) _____ deer ate leaves from the branch.

5. The (scurry) _____ ants are all over the grass.

▷ Revisit a piece of your writing. Edit the draft to make sure present participles are used correctly.

Past Participles

The **past participle** of regular verbs is formed by adding –*ed* to the verb. If the verb ends in *e,* drop the *e* before adding –*ed*. If the verb ends in *y,* drop the *y* and add –*ied*.

> mix + ed = mixed
> store + ed = stored
> study + ed = studied

Remember that the **participle** form of a verb can be used as an adjective.

> Workers moved the **stored** boxes to a new warehouse.

> **On the line, write the past participle form of the verb shown in parentheses.**

1. The (stuff) _____ box was filled with puppy toys.

2. The (tire) _____ puppy took a nap.

3. Trish carefully carried the (rescue) _____ kitten in her arms.

4. Carlos disposed of the (ruin) _____ carpet.

5. The (rest) _____ kitten yawned and opened its eyes.

> **Revisit a piece of your writing. Edit the draft to make sure past participles are used correctly.**

Participial Phrases

> A **participial phrase** begins with a participle and describes a noun. Participial phrases are formed using past and present participles.
>
> > The children playing with the puppy laughed with joy.
> > Mariella returned to find her picnic lunch covered with ants.

▶ **Underline the participial phrase in each sentence. Then, circle the subject it modifies.**

1. The sea turtles shuffling across the sand move toward the ocean.

2. The family sitting on the blanket is having a picnic.

3. Pablo saw a ship encrusted with barnacles.

4. The beach covered with seashells was a fun place to visit.

5. The ball bouncing along the ground belongs to me.

▶ **Revisit a piece of your writing. Edit the draft to make sure participial phrases are used correctly.**

Review Participles

A **present participle** is a verb form that ends in *-ing*. A
present participle can be used as an adjective.

A **past participle** is a verb form that can also be used as
an adjective. Most past participles end in *-d* or *-ed*.
Some irregular verbs have special past participle forms.

A **participial phrase** contains a present or past
participle and other accompanying words. A participial
phrase can be used to modify a subject.

> **Circle the participle in each sentence. Then write on the line whether it is a
present or past participle. If the participle is part of a participial phrase, underline
the phrase.**

1. The burned pizza did not taste very good. _____

2. The students practicing for the talent show are in the gym. _____

3. Carlota wrote in a notebook plastered with stickers. _____

4. The teachers sitting in the lounge discuss current events. _____

5. The audience amazed by the play clapped loudly. _____

> **Revisit a piece of your writing. Edit the draft to make sure participles and
participial phrases are used correctly.**

Connect to Writing: Using Participles

> **Read the selection and choose the best answer to each question.**

Read the following paragraph about a science class exploring the trees in the park. Look for any revisions that should be made. Then answer the questions that follow.

    (1) The students studied trees in the park. (2) They gathered leaves to examine. (3) They were going to have a test over their studies. (4) Dana was worried about failing the test. (5) She studied for an extra hour. (6) Checking the time, the teacher hurried to finish the lesson.

1. What changes can be made to combine sentences 1 and 2 using a participial phrase?

  A. The students studying trees in the park and they gathered leaves to examine.

  B. The students studying trees in the park and gathering leaves to examine.

  C. The students studying trees in the park gathered leaves to examine.

  D. The students studied trees in the park as they gathered leaves to examine.

2. What changes can be made to combine sentences 3 and 4 using a participial phrase?

  A. Worrying about failing the test, Dana studied for an extra hour.

  B. Worried about failing the test, Dana studied for an extra hour.

  C. Dana was worried about failing the test, but she studied for an extra hour.

  D. Dana was worried about failing the test because she studied for an extra hour.

> **Write about a special project or activity that you have done at school. Be sure to use participial phrases in your writing.**

_____

_____

_____

_____

_____

Adjectives

> An **adjective** is a word that gives information about a noun or pronoun. Choose adjectives carefully to describe nouns.
>
> Adjectives often tell *what kind, how many*, or *which one*. An adjective typically comes before the noun that it describes.
>
> The <u>large</u> crowd gathered to hear the speech. (adjective; *what kind*)

▶ **Identify the adjectives that describe the underlined nouns. Then tell if the adjective indicates what kind, which one, or how many.**

1. She wore a purple <u>coat</u> and a wool <u>hat</u>. _____

2. The red <u>car</u> left the parking lot first. _____

3. She lost her new <u>phone</u>. _____

4. The class has nineteen <u>students</u>. _____

5. We watched a funny <u>movie</u> last night. _____

▶ **Revisit a piece of your writing. Edit the draft to make sure adjectives are used correctly.**

Adjectives After *Be*

An **adjective** is a word that gives information about a noun or pronoun. Adjectives do not always occur near the noun or pronoun they describe. The adjective can come after a form of the verb *be* (*am/was, are/were,* and *is/was*) in a sentence.

The sky <u>was gloomy</u>. (*was* – form of verb *be*; *gloomy* – adjective)

> **Underline the adjective. Then write the word it describes on the line.**

1. The wind was cool. _____

2. She is excited to ride the train. _____

3. The sun was bright this morning. _____

4. The team was anxious to play the game. _____

5. The coach was confident. _____

6. We were tired from the journey. _____

7. The road is icy. _____

8. The valley is foggy. _____

9. The puppy is excited. _____

10. I am warm under the blanket. _____

> **Revisit a piece of your writing. Edit the draft to make sure adjectives after the verb *be* are used correctly.**

Ordering Adjectives

An **adjective** is a word that gives information about a noun or pronoun. Sometimes a writer uses more than one adjective to describe a noun. When this is done, the adjectives should be in a certain order. That order is generally *number, opinion, size, shape, age, color, material,* and *purpose.*

There are <u>fifteen ugly, green</u> frogs in the pond.

> **Read the sentences. Combine the adjectives in the correct order and write them on the line.**

1. There are bicycles outside. They are blue. They are small. There are four of them.
   There are _____ bicycles outside.

2. She likes the earrings the best. They are red. They are beautiful. They are square.
   She likes the _____ earrings best.

3. The sweaters are on sale. They are striped. There are ten of them.
   The _____ sweaters are on sale.

4. The jockey is an athlete. She is slim. The jockey is skillful.
   The jockey is a _____ athlete.

5. The cars are parked in the driveway. The cars are green. There are three of them.
   The _____ cars are parked in the driveway.

> **Revisit a piece of your writing. Edit the draft to make sure adjectives are ordered correctly.**

Review Adjectives

An **adjective** is a word that gives information about a noun or pronoun. Choose adjectives carefully to describe nouns exactly. An adjective can tell *what kind, which one*, or *how many*.

Adjectives often appear before the nouns they describe. An adjective can follow the word it describes. This usually happens when an adjective follows a form of the verb *be*.

Sometimes a writer uses more than one adjective to describe a noun. When this is done, the adjectives should be in a certain order. That order is generally *number, opinion, size, shape, age, color, material,* and *purpose*.

> **Identify all of the adjectives in each sentence.**

1. Uncle Bob's antique car was beautiful. _____

2. She is wearing a pink dress that is very sparkly. _____

3. My older brother is generous. _____

4. We put colorful flowers on the tables. _____

5. The guide on our tour was informative and helpful. _____

> **Put the adjectives in these sentences in the correct order.**

6. The woman drove a black beautiful car. _____

7. The blue tiny six marbles rolled off the table. _____

8. My winter puffy coat is hanging in the closet. _____

9. The coach gave spirited three speeches to the team this year. _____

10. The two brown tired puppies napped on the cushion. _____

> **Revisit a piece of your writing. Edit the draft to make sure adjectives are used correctly.**

Connect to Writing: Using Adjectives

> **Read the selection and choose the best answer to each question.**

Read the following paragraph about visiting an aquarium. Look for any revisions that should be made. Then answer the questions that follow.

    (1) Our class took a field trip to an aquarium. (2) We saw many small fish in one tank. (3) The fish were blue. (4) We also watched playful three beautiful dolphins put on a water show. (5) We all had a wonderful time at the aquarium. (6) I can't wait for our next field trip!

1. How should sentences 2 and 3 be combined so the adjectives are in the correct order?

    A. We saw small blue many fish in one tank.

    B. We saw many blue small fish in one tank.

    C. We saw many small blue fish in one tank.

    D. We saw blue many small fish in one tank.

2. What changes can be made in sentence 4 so the adjectives are in the correct order?

    A. We also watched beautiful, playful three dolphins put on a water show.

    B. We also watched playful, beautiful, three dolphins put on a water show.

    C. We also watched three beautiful, playful dolphins put on a water show.

    D. Make no changes.

> **Write about a class field trip you have taken in the past or an upcoming field trip. Be sure to use plenty of adjectives and make sure they are ordered correctly.**

_____

_____

_____

_____

Adverbs

An **adverb** is a word that tells something about a verb. Choose adverbs carefully to describe the verb exactly. Some adverbs tell *how, when,* or *where.* An adverb can come before or after the verb. Most adverbs that tell *how* end in *-ly.* The adverbs in this sentence tell about the verb *played.*

> **when   how   where**
> Yesterday, Kristin played happily outside.

▶ **The verb in each sentence is underlined. Write the adverb. Then write whether it tells *how, when,* or *where.***

1. Students <u>walked</u> confidently across the stage. _____

2. Ian eventually <u>became</u> friends with Calvin. _____

3. Tina <u>taught</u> her dog to sit there. _____

4. Suddenly, Stephanie <u>hugged</u> her mom. _____

5. The cat playfully <u>pounced</u> on the toy. _____

▶ **Underline each adverb. Write the verb it describes.**

6. Someday our dog will learn how to behave. _____

7. Tonya gently held the kitten. _____

8. Diego quickly typed on the keyboard. _____

9. Mom put the puppy outside. _____

10. Ava's friends laughed loudly at her joke. _____

▶ **Revisit a piece of your writing. Edit the draft to make sure adverbs are used correctly.**

Adverbs of Frequency and Intensity

An **adverb** is a word that tells something about a verb.

Adverbs of frequency tell how often an action happens.

> My mom <u>usually</u> wakes at 5 A.M.

Adverbs of intensity tell how much or to what degree an action happens.

> She was tired, but she <u>hardly</u> slept.

▶ **Underline the adverb in each sentence, and circle the verb it describes. Write whether the adverb tells *how often* or *how much*.**

1. Tómas always eats an apple during lunch. _____

2. Tiffany almost missed the bus for school. _____

3. My dog follows me a lot. _____

4. Angela usually goes to the library after school. _____

5. Our cat never plays with our dog. _____

▶ **Revisit a piece of your writing. Edit the draft to make sure adverbs that tell *how often* and *how much* are used correctly.**

Adverbs in Different Parts of Sentences

An **adverb** is a word that tells something about a verb. Adverbs often follow the verb, but adverbs can be used at the beginning, middle, or end of a sentence.

> **adverb: carefully**
> <u>Carefully</u>, Mrs. Gonzalez trained her service dog.
> Mrs. Gonzalez <u>carefully</u> trained her service dog.
> Mrs. Gonzalez trained her service dog <u>carefully</u>.

> **Underline the adverb in each sentence, and circle the verb it describes. Write whether the adverb is used at the beginning, middle, or end of the sentence.**

1. Usually, Alejandro reads during lunch. _____

2. The students sat quietly at their desks. _____

3. She thinks about her dog a lot. _____

4. Sometimes, the teacher quizzes students after they read. _____

5. The kitten pounced on the toy quickly. _____

> **Revisit a piece of your writing. Edit the draft to make sure adverbs are used correctly.**

Review Adverbs

An **adverb** is a word that tells something about a verb. Some adverbs tell *when*, *where*, or *how* about a verb. Most adverbs that tell how end in *-ly*.
Adverbs of frequency tell how often an action happens.
Adverbs of intensity tell how much or to what degree an action happens.
An adverb can be used anywhere in a sentence. It can come at the beginning, middle, or end.

> **Write the adverb in each sentence. Then underline the verb it describes.**

1. The group sang loudly at the concert. _____

2. The man ran daily with his dog. _____

3. Gracefully, the dancers moved across the stage. _____

4. The train traveled northward. _____

5. The baby looked up at me curiously. _____

> **Revisit a piece of your writing. Edit the draft to make sure adverbs are used correctly.**

Connect to Writing: Using Adverbs

▸ **Read the selection and choose the best answer to each question.**

Read the following paragraph about swimming at the lake during the summer. Look for any revisions that should be made. Then answer the questions that follow.

(1) We awoke as the sun began to rise over the lake. (2) We stepped out of our tents. (3) The sun shined brightly in our faces, causing us to squint. (4) The day was already hot, and the water looked inviting. (5) We couldn't wait to swim in the lake! (6) My older brother raced to the shore and jumped in. (7) The rest of us jumped in after him. (8) We all had a wonderful day at the lake!

1. What change can be made to sentence 3 using a more precise adverb?

   A. Change *brightly* to *glowingly.*

   B. Change *shined* to *gleamed.*

   C. Change *brightly* to *blindingly.*

   D. Change *shined* to *beamed.*

2. What change can be made to sentence 6 using an adverb to make the writing more precise?

   A. My older brother swiftly raced to the shore and jumped in.

   B. Slowly, my older brother raced to the shore and jumped in.

   C. My older brother raced fast to the shore and jumped in.

   D. Quick my older brother was, and he raced to the shore and jumped in.

▸ **Write about a favorite vacation or family outing that you have had. Be sure to use precise adverbs in your writing.**

_____

_____

_____

_____

Clauses

A **clause** is a group of words that has a subject and predicate but may or may not stand alone.

A clause that can stand alone because it is a complete sentence is called an **independent clause**.

A clause that cannot stand alone because it is not a complete sentence is called a **dependent clause**.

Independent Clause	Dependent Clause

We always buy milk, eggs, and bread <u>when we go to the grocery store.</u>

▶ **Identify the clause in each sentence that is in parentheses.**

1. Since the day was cold and cloudy, we went to the movies. (independent)

   _____

2. We sat in the seats that no one else wanted. (dependent)

   _____

3. After we parked the car, we bought our tickets. (dependent)

   _____

4. The audience cheered when the movie ended. (independent)

   _____

5. The sun was shining when we left the theater. (dependent)

   _____

▶ **Revisit a piece of your writing. Edit the draft to make sure clauses are used correctly.**

Relative Pronouns

A **relative pronoun** stands for a noun and introduces a dependent clause that tells about the noun. The pronoun refers back to the noun it stands for.

I know the man <u>who</u> works here. (relative pronoun)

▷ **For each sentence, circle the relative pronoun and underline the dependent clause. Then write the noun this clause describes on the line.**

1. On Saturday, we went to a beach that has white sand.

_____

2. My friends, who live near a state park, go hiking every weekend.

_____

3. My favorite author wrote this book, which tells about a kingdom from long ago.

_____

4. We took Ava, whose family just moved to town, to the library.

_____

5. Therese went to the movie theater that is near her neighborhood.

_____

▷ **Revisit a piece of your writing. Edit the draft to make sure relative pronouns are used correctly.**

Relative Adverbs

A **relative adverb** introduces a dependent clause that tells about a place, a time, or a reason.

This is the path <u>where</u> we'll begin our journey. (tells about a place)

> **Identify the relative adverb in each sentence below.**

1. I am not sure why Tom got so upset. _____

2. I will never forget when I saw the concert in Colorado. _____

3. Earth Day is the time when we remember to care for our planet. _____

4. They planted a garden where the swing set once was. _____

5. I can tell you why we celebrate this holiday each year. _____

> **Revisit a piece of your writing. Edit the draft to make sure relative adverbs are used correctly.**

Review Relative Pronouns and Adverbs

A **relative pronoun** stands for a noun and introduces a dependent clause that tells about the noun. The pronoun refers back to the noun it stands for.
A **relative adverb** introduces a dependent clause that tells about a place, a time, or a reason.

> Circle the relative pronoun or relative adverb that begins a dependent clause. Then underline the dependent clause

1. Tacos, which we always have on Tuesday, are my favorite family meal.

2. I am looking for someone who can teach me to speak French.

3. There must be a reason why Shelly cried at recess.

4. The dress that Rhi wore to the dance was pale pink.

5. This past summer Maddie set up a lemonade stand that was very successful.

> Revisit a piece of your writing. Edit the draft to make sure relative pronouns and adverbs are used correctly.

Connect to Writing: Using Relative Pronouns and Adverbs

> **Read the selection and choose the best answer to each question.**

Read the following paragraph about getting a new aquarium. Look for any revisions that should be made. Then answer the questions that follow.

(1) That was the day. (2) The new fish arrived. (3) The fish were put in the large aquarium, where they could swim all around. (4) The fish hid under the coral arch, which provided safety. (5) Later, they swam to the surface. (6) Their food was scattered there on the water.

1. How can you combine sentences 1 and 2 using relative pronouns and adverbs to show how ideas are connected?

    A. That was the day new fish arrived.

    B. That was the day the new fish arrived.

    C. That was the day when the new fish arrived.

    D. That was the day we got new fish.

2. How can you combine sentences 5 and 6 using relative pronouns and adverbs to show how ideas are connected?

    A. Later, they swam to the surface, where their food was scattered on the water.

    B. Later, they swam to the surface, their food was there.

    C. Later, they swam to the surface and ate their food.

    D. Later, they swam to the surface to eat their food.

> **Write about a pet you have or a pet you'd like to have. Be sure to use relative pronouns and adverbs to connect your ideas.**

_____

_____

_____

Comparative Forms of Adjectives

A **comparative adjective** compares two things, places, or people. Many comparative adjectives end in -*er*.

slow–slower
A snail is **slower** than a cheetah. (comparative form)

▶ **Write the comparative form of each adjective in parentheses to complete each sentence.**

1. His car is _____ than mine. (loud)

2. My sister's room is _____ than my brother's room. (clean)

3. Checkers is _____ to learn than chess. (easy)

4. After working all day, Stan is _____ than ever! (grumpy)

5. She ran _____ today than she did yesterday. (fast)

▶ **Revisit a piece of your writing. Edit the draft to make sure comparative forms of adjectives are used correctly.**

Superlative Forms of Adjectives

> A **superlative adjective** compares more than two things, places, or people. Many superlative adjectives end in *-est*.
>
> *slow–slowest*
> A sloth is the **slowest** of them all. (superlative form)

▶ **Write the superlative of each adjective in parentheses to complete each sentence.**

1. The alligator was the _____ reptile I saw at the zoo. (scary)

2. The Miller family has the _____ garden in the neighborhood. (pretty)

3. Carrie has the _____ dog on the block. (small)

4. Anabel thought her grandma was the _____ person in the world. (nice)

5. Jorge was the _____ runner on the track today. (fast)

▶ **Revisit a piece of your writing. Edit the draft to make sure superlative forms of adjectives are used correctly.**

Comparative and Superlative Forms of Adverbs

A **comparative adverb** compares the action of two or more things. The word *more* is often used. A **comparative adjective** compares two things, places, or people. Many comparative adjectives end in *-er*. A **superlative adverb** compares the action of more than two things. The word *most* is often used. A **superlative adjective** compares more than two things, places, or people. Many superlative adjectives end in *-est*.

Adverb	Comparative	Superlative
slowly	more slowly	most slowly
soon	sooner	soonest
prompt	more promptly	most promptly

▶ **Use a comparative or superlative adverb for each blank below. Use the word bank to help you complete the sentences.**

louder	more quickly	closer	more completely	harder
loudest	most quickly	closest	most completely	hardest

1. Although many musicians were loud, Donald played the trumpet
   _____ .

2. Sarah could add numbers _____ than her brother.

3. Of all my friends, Carmen lives _____ .

4. Marty worked _____ on the project than his partner.

5. Jeremy answered the question _____ of the three contestants.

▶ **Revisit a piece of your writing. Edit the draft to make sure comparative and superlative forms of adverbs are used correctly.**

Review Comparative and Superlative Adjectives and Adverbs

> - A **comparative adjective** compares two people, places, or things.
> - A **superlative adjective** compares more than two people, places, or things.
> - **Adverbs** also have comparative and superlative forms.

> **▷ Underline the correct choice to complete each sentence correctly.**

1. In his room, the television is turned up (more loudly, most loudly) than the stereo.

2. My dog has the (softer, softest) fur I've ever felt.

3. Rose is the (kinder, kindest) person I have ever met.

4. The puppies are (smaller, smallest) than I thought they would be.

5. My mom sings (more beautifully, most beautifully) of all the members in the choir.

> **▷ Revisit a piece of your writing. Edit the draft to make sure comparative and superlative adjectives and adverbs are used correctly.**

Connect to Writing: Using Comparative and Superlative Adjectives and Adverbs

> Read the selection and choose the best answer to each question.

Read the following paragraph about hiking in the woods. Look for any revisions that should be made. Then answer the questions that follow.

(1) On Sunday, we drove to the state park to go hiking. (2) It was a hot day! (3) We found our trail. (4) It was a long trail, not like the one we hiked last week. (5) We hiked into the evening and used the North Star to guide us back to our car. (6) The star shined brightly in the night sky.

1. How can you change sentence 4 using a comparative adjective?

    A. It was the longest trail we have ever hiked.

    B. It was a longer trail than the one we hiked last week.

    C. It was a long, long trail and not like the one we hiked last week.

    D. It was a very long trail, not like the one we hiked last week.

2. How can you change sentence 6 using a superlative adverb?

    A. The star shined most brightly among the stars in the night sky.

    B. The star shined more bright among the stars in the night sky.

    C. The star shined brightliest among the stars in the night sky.

    D. The star shined most brightlier among the stars in the night sky.

> Write about a time you have hiked, camped, or played in the park with your friends or family. Be sure to use comparative and superlative adjectives and adverbs in your writing.

_____

_____

_____

_____

Making Comparisons

Comparative adjectives are used to compare two things.
Superlative adjectives are used to compare more than two things.

Adjective	Comparative	Superlative
fast	faster	fastest
smart	smarter	smartest
cold	colder	coldest
sad	sadder	saddest

A zebra is **faster** than a turtle.

A cheetah is the **fastest** animal.

> Circle the correct form of the adjective to complete each sentence. Write C if the adjective is the comparative form. Write S if the adjective is the superlative form.

1. Sarah is (short, shorter) than her sister. _____

2. Jean's hands are (colder, coldest) than Maya's. _____

3. The snow at the hill is (deep, deeper) than the snow in our backyard. _____

4. Colorado has the (deeper, deepest) snow. _____

5. That was the (sadder, saddest) movie I have ever seen. _____

> Revisit a piece of your writing. Edit the draft to make sure that you are making comparisons correctly.

Making Comparisons with *More* and *Most*

> With long adjectives, use *more* to compare two persons, places, or things.
> Use *most* to compare three or more.
>
> The monarch butterfy is **more colorful** than the moth.
> The parrot is the **most colorful** bird in the jungle.

> **Complete each sentence, adding either *more* or *most* to the adjective in parentheses.**

1. The _____ movies are about things you wouldn't expect.
   (interesting)

2. The _____ dress in the store is the one in the corner with red
   beads. (elegant)

3. The small screwdriver is _____ than the large one. (useful)

4. The green ski jacket is _____ than the white jacket, against
   the snow. (visible)

5. The icy driving conditions are the _____ part of the snowstorm.
   (dangerous)

> **Revisit a piece of your writing. Edit the draft to make sure that you are writing comparisons with *more* and *most* correctly.**

Comparing with *Good* and *Bad*

Some adjectives need to change forms when they are used to compare things. The adjectives *good* and *bad* are two examples.

Adjective	Comparative	Superlative
Good	Better	Best
Bad	Worse	Worst

Winning third place is **good**. Coming in second is **better**. Winning first prize is **best!**

▶ **Complete each sentence by writing the correct form of the adjective shown in parentheses.**

1. My mom says that reading is a _____ way to spend your time than playing video games. (good)

2. Chicago deep-dish is the _____ type of pizza! (good)

3. Not doing your homework is _____ than forgetting it at home. (bad)

4. Having the stomach flu is the _____ way to spend your birthday. (bad)

5. Since she went to the doctor, her symptoms are _____. (good)

▶ **Revisit a piece of your writing. Edit the draft to make sure that you are making comparisons with *good* and *bad* correctly.**

Review Making Comparisons

Comparative adjectives are used to compare two things.
Superlative adjectives are used to compare more than two things.

With long adjectives, use *more* to compare two persons, places, or things. Use *most* to compare three or more.

Some adjectives like *good* and *bad* need to change forms when they are used to compare things.

▷ **Complete the sentence by writing the correct form of the adjective shown in parentheses.**

1. The _____ part of the Mediterranean Sea is 17,280 feet. (deep)

2. The Dead Sea is much _____ than the Mediterranean Sea. (shallow)

3. The Dead Sea is the _____ body of water in the world. (salty)

4. The Carribbean Sea is much _____ than the Arctic Ocean. (warm)

5. The weather during the second week was _____ than the first week. (good)

▷ **Revisit a piece of your writing. Edit the draft to make sure that you are writing comparative adjectives correctly.**

Connect to Writing: Using Comparisons

> **Read the selection and choose the best answer to each question.**

Sam wrote the following paragraph about the geography unit his class just completed. Read his paragraph and look for revisions he should make. Then answer the questions that follow.

(1) Of the seven continents on Earth, Asia is the larger. (2) South America is slightly smaller than North America. (3) Asia is more populous than South America. (4) The biggest desert in the world is in Africa. (5) Flying is a better way to travel across Asia than driving.

1. Which statement is not written correctly?

  A. Of the seven continents on Earth, Asia is the larger.

  B. South America is slightly smaller than North America.

  C. Asia is more populous than South America.

  D. Flying is a better way to travel across Asia than driving.

2. Which sentence correctly uses a superlative adjective?

  A. Asia is more populous than South America.

  B. South America is slightly smaller than North America.

  C. The biggest desert in the world is in Africa.

  D. Flying is a better way to travel across Asia than driving.

> **Where would you like to visit? Write a few sentences about what you would expect to see, using comparative and superlative adjectives.**

_____

_____

_____

_____

Prepositions

A **preposition** is a word that shows a connection between other words in a sentence. Some prepositions describe time and others describe place.

This show is **about** ocean life.

▶ **Write the preposition in each underlined prepositional phrase.**

1. Tom believes that his team can beat the other team <u>without any effort</u>. _____

2. The race is <u>between the tortoise and the hare</u>. _____

3. Tom is thrilled when his team is <u>near the home stretch</u>. _____

4. The race car gains speed <u>along the straight away</u>. _____

5. The cheers could be heard <u>from the stands</u>. _____

▶ **Revisit a piece of your writing. Edit the draft to make sure that your prepositions are written correctly.**

Prepositional Phrases

> A **prepositional phrase** begins with a preposition and ends with a noun or a pronoun. These words and all the words in between them make up the prepositional phrase.
>
> The bird ate a few worms **for** his breakfast.

▶ **In each sentence below, write the prepositional phrase on the line. Then underline the preposition in the sentence.**

1. The sun emerged over the horizon. _____

2. The mother bird keeps her eggs in a safe spot. _____

3. Polar bears sometimes swim in the ocean. _____

4. There are many campers around the campfire. _____

5. The cars were let through the campground gate. _____

▶ **Revisit a piece of your writing. Edit the draft to make sure that your prepositional phrases are written correctly.**

Prepositional Phrases to Provide Details

A **prepositional phrase** begins with a preposition and ends with a noun or a pronoun. These words and all the words in between them make up the prepositional phrase.

A prepositional phrase can give more details in a sentence. A prepositional phrase can tell where, when, or how.

> **How**: Seagulls scoop up fish with their beak.
> **Where**: They catch them in the ocean.
> **When**: They do most of their fishing in the morning.

▶ Identify the prepositional phrase in each sentence. Does the prepositional phrase tell how, where, or when?

1. The temperatures can be lower in the evening. _____

2. The crabs catch their food with their claws. _____

3. The groundhogs burrow into the dirt. _____

4. They started driving in the morning as the sun came up. _____

5. The groundhog burrows cannot be seen from the house. _____

▶ Revisit a piece of your writing. Edit the draft to make sure that your prepositional phrases are written correctly.

Review Prepositions and Prepositional Phrases

A **preposition** is a word that shows a connection between other words in a sentence.

A **prepositional phrase** begins with a preposition and ends with a noun or a pronoun. These words and all the words in between them make up the prepositional phrase.

A prepositional phrase can give more details in a sentence. A prepositional phrase can tell where, when, or how.

> The water gives them relief **from the heat**. (*from the heat* is the prepositional phrase)
>
> Mike sometimes goes swimming **after work**. (*after work* is the prepositional phrase)

> Identify the prepositional phrase in each sentence.

1. Dan has a job working on the railroad line. _____

2. Skip likes working with cars and motorcycles. _____

3. In the summer, she is going to lifeguard. _____

4. The shade tree gave the dogs relief from the heat. _____

5. It is hot; Anna brought extra water with her. _____

> Revisit a piece of your writing. Edit the draft to make sure that your prepositional phrases are written correctly.

Connect to Writing: Using Prepositions and Prepositional Phrases

> **Read the selection and choose the best answer to each question.**

Read the following paragraph about driving to a relative's house for a family birthday. Look for any revisions that should be made. Then answer the questions that follow.

(1) We woke up early. (2) We are driving to my cousin's house for her birthday party. (3) It was a long drive and I was excited to arrive. (4) There was a piñata and birthday cake outside on the deck. (5) We sang "Happy Birthday" and my cousin opened her presents. (6) She loved the gift we brought her. (7) After cake and presents, we took turns with the piñata. (8) It was a great day!

1. How can you change sentence 1 using a preposition or prepositional phrase?

   A. We woke up really early.

   B. We woke up extremely early.

   C. We woke up early in the morning.

   D. Make no changes.

2. How can you change sentence 5 using a preposition or prepositional phrase?

   A. We sang "Happy Birthday," so my cousin opened her presents.

   B. We sang "Happy Birthday," and my cousin opened her presents.

   C. My cousin opened her presents after we sang "Happy Birthday."

   D. Make no changes.

> **Write about a weekend or a special time that you spent with your family. Be sure to include prepositions or prepositional phrases in your writing.**

_____

_____

_____

_____

Contractions with *Not*

> A **negative** is a word that makes a sentence mean *no*.
>
> A **negative contraction** is made with a verb and the negative word *not*.
>
> An apostrophe takes the place of the letter *o* in each contraction with *not*.
>
> **contraction with *not***
> Bob **isn't** at school, but he may be home sick.

> **Write the contraction for the underlined word or words in each sentence.**

1. Jan <u>was not</u> the last one to arrive at the party. _____

2. She <u>does not</u> know why it took so long to get there. _____

3. Kate's skates from last year <u>will not</u> fit her this year. _____

4. There <u>were not</u> many people at the skating rink today. _____

5. Sarah <u>cannot</u> find her gloves, and her hands are cold! _____

6. Please <u>do not</u> tell me she left them at the movies yesterday. _____

7. Jack <u>did not</u> want to go because he was tired. _____

8. Allison <u>had not</u> arrived yet when we got there. _____

9. We <u>cannot</u> see the sign from the road. _____

10. The school <u>does not</u> serve lunch today. _____

> **Revisit a piece of your writing. Edit the draft to make sure that your contractions with *not* are written correctly.**

Grammar
5.1.2

Using Negatives

The words *no, no one, nobody, none, nothing, nowhere,* and *never* are negatives.

A contraction with a verb and the word *not* is also a negative. When making a negative statement, make sure to use just one negative.

positive
I like chocolate cake.
negative
I **don't** like chocolate cake.
I like **none** of the cakes that are chocolate.

> Use a negative to change the meaning of the sentence from positive to negative. Write the negative sentence on the line below.

1. Sarah likes science class.

_____

2. The experiments we do in science class are dangerous!

_____

3. I always wear goggles to protect my eyes.

_____

4. Everyone enjoys working as a group in science class.

_____

5. We were excited to move to the next unit: physics.

_____

> Revisit a piece of your writing. Edit the draft to make sure that negatives are written correctly.

Grade 4 • Negatives
© Houghton Mifflin Harcourt Publishing Company. All rights reserved.
Printable
112

Avoiding Double Negatives

Words such as *not, no,* and *never* are negatives. Using two negatives together is called a double negative. Never use two negatives together in a sentence.

> **double negative**
> Frank won't tell nobody what score he got on his test.
> **corrected sentences**
> Frank won't tell anybody what score he got on his test.
> Frank will tell nobody what score he got on his test.

> Write the correct word shown in parentheses to complete the sentence.

1. There (isn't, is) no reason to worry about the weather this weekend. _____

2. There isn't (anything, nothing) we need at the grocery store. _____

3. We haven't eaten (any, none) of the food we bought the other day. _____

4. There isn't going to be (any, no) more snow tomorrow. _____

5. We won't have trouble driving (anywhere, nowhere) tomorrow. _____

> Revisit a piece of your writing. Edit the draft to make sure that you have avoided using any double negatives.

Review Negatives

A **negative** is a word that makes a sentence mean *no*.

A **negative contraction** is made with a verb and the negative word *not*. An apostrophe takes the place of the letter o in each contraction with *not*.

The words *no, not, no one, nobody, none, nothing, nowhere,* and *never* are negatives. Using two negatives together is called a **double negative**. Never use two negatives together in a sentence.

> Use a negative to change the meaning of the sentence from positive to negative. Write the negative sentence on the line below.

1. Jim has chosen a puppy from the litter.

_____

2. She is ready to leave her mother and go to her new home.

_____

3. The new puppy will love travelling in the car to her new home.

_____

> Write the correct word shown in parentheses to complete the sentence.

4. There (is, isn't) no way I'm going to miss the big game tonight.   _____

5. There won't be (anyone, no one) collecting tickets at the door.   _____

> Revisit a piece of your writing. Edit the draft to make sure that you have written negatives correctly.

Connect to Writing: Using Negatives

> **Read the selection and choose the best answer to each question.**

Elsa wrote the following paragraph about her plans for the coming summer vacation.
Read her paragraph and look for revisions she should make. Then answer the questions
that follow.

(1) Elsa could not be happer that summer is approaching! (2) She has not had no free time during the school year. (3) She is really looking forward to not having any work to do. (4) She is not going to stay inside—she plans to play outside every day. (5) She wants to keep busy.

1. Which statement is not written correctly?

   A. Elsa could not be happer that summer is approaching!

   B. She has not had no free time during the school year.

   C. She is really looking forward to not having any work to do.

   D. She is not going to stay inside—she plans to play outside every day.

2. Which statement is a proper negative form of statement 5?

   A. She wants to not keep busy.

   B. She doesn't want to keep busy.

   C. She doesn't want to do nothing.

   D. She wants to not be not busy.

> **What are your plans for this summer? Write two or three sentences about it.**

_____

_____

_____

_____

Quotation Marks with Direct Speech

A **quotation** is made up of the exact words that someone has said. Use quotation marks (" ") before and after the quotation.

Always capitalize the first word of a quotation and use correct end punctuation. When the quotation begins a sentence, use a comma at the end of the statement unless it is a question or an exclamation. If the speaker's name begins a sentence, use a comma after *said*.

"I hope Sarah can come for a visit," said Juan.
Juan said, "I'm going to take him on a tour of the neighborhood."

▸ **Write each sentence correctly. Capitalize words that should be capitalized. Add quotation marks, commas, and end marks where they are needed.**

1. summer vacation is almost here said Juan

   _____

2. Sarah said it's going to be great sleeping late in the morning

   _____

3. we are going to swim every day said Jessica

   _____

4. Juan said as long as it doesn't rain

   _____

5. they are going to join us soon said Sarah

   _____

▸ **Revisit a piece of your writing. Edit the draft to make sure that quotations used with direct speech are written with correct capitalization and punctuation.**

Split Quotations

Sometimes the words that tell who is speaking come in the middle of a quotation.

If the first part of the quotation is a complete sentence, use a comma before and then a period after the words that tell who is speaking. Capitalize the first letter in the second sentence of the quotation.

> "I lived near the North Pole," said Dad. "There were no libraries nearby."

If the entire quotation is one sentence, use a comma after the words that tell who is speaking. Do not capitalize the first letter in the second part of the quotation.

> "I love to read," he said, "so I found ways to get books."

> **Write the quotations correctly.**

1. I love to swim exclaimed Jenna I am going to swim every day.

   _____

2. I'm going to try out for the swim team said Jenna they practice every morning.

   _____

3. I'll get a good night's sleep explained Jenna so I wont be tired for morning practice.

   _____

4. Can I come see your swim meets asked Anna I'll cheer for you.

   _____

5. We all want to get some ice cream said Anna. Can you come with us?

   _____

> **Revisit a piece of your writing. Edit the draft to make sure that your split quotations are written correctly.**

Quotations from Text

For a report, you might use a quotation from a text. Use the same punctuation and capitalization rules that you use for other quotations. The name of the book or author that the quotation comes from is called the source. Be sure to include the source. Be sure to use the source's exact words.

Original text: "English Bulldogs are known for their loyalty to their owners."
Source: The Encyclopedia of Dogs

quotation from text:
According to The Encyclopedia of Dogs, "English Bulldogs are known for their loyalty to their owners."

Original text: "English Bulldogs often sit by the door, waiting for their owners to return home."
Source: author James West

quotation from text:
"English Bulldogs often sit by the door, waiting for their owners to return home," writes James West.

> **Write the quotations correctly.**

1. Quotation: "The Komodo dragon is the world's largest lizard."
   Source: Apex Predators

   _____

   _____

2. Quotation: "Flowers on the Spiderwort plant change colors depending on the levels of pollution in the air."
   Source: authors Mary Pope Osborne and Natalie Pope Boyce

   _____

   _____

> **Revisit a piece of your writing. Edit the draft to make sure that your quotations from text are written correctly.**

Review Quotations

Always capitalize the first word of a quotation and use correct end punctuation. If the speaker's name begins a sentence, use a comma after *said*.

Sometimes the words that tell who is speaking come in the middle of a quotation.

For a report, you might use a quotation from a text. Use the same punctuation and capitalization rules that you use for other quotations. Be sure to include the source. Be sure to use the source's exact words.

> Write the quotations correctly.

1. The blue team is up first tonight said Jane.

   _____

2. Let's get there early said Marty I want to have time to warm up before our game.

   _____

3. Is Coach Keyes bringing snacks asked mom if not I'll make some for the team.

   _____

4. He said he'd bring snacks said Jane.

   _____

> Write the following quotation from text correctly.

5. Quotation: "We measure space by the distance light travels in one year."
   Source: "The Magic Treehouse Incredible Fact Book"

   _____

   _____

> Revisit a piece of your writing. Edit the draft to make sure that your quotations are written correctly.

Connect to Writing: Using Quotations

> **Read the selection and choose the best answer to each question.**

David wrote the following paragraph about a conversation he had with his school librarian. Read his paragraph and look for revisions he should make. Then answer the questions that follow.

(1) "Hi Ms. Lack," said David, "I'm looking for a book about life in outer space." (2) Let me see what we have said Ms. Lack. (3) "Here's a book that might help, she said. "It was just returned." (4) We have never been closer to discovering life in space, the authors write. (5) "The discovery of water on Mars is the first step to finding life forms," according to Recent Developments in Space Research.

1. Which version of statement 2 uses quotation marks properly?

   A. Let me see what we have said Ms. Lack.

   B. "Let me see what we have said Ms. Lack."

   C. "Let me see what we have," said Ms. Lack.

   D. "Let me see" what we have said Ms. Lack.

2. Which statement properly quotes a source book?

   A. "Here's a book that might help," she said. "It was just returned."

   B. "Hi Ms. Lack," said David, "I'm looking for a book about life in outer space."

   C. We have never been closer to discovering life in space, the authors write.

   D. "The discovery of water on Mars is the first step to finding life forms," according to Recent Developments in Space Research.

> **Do you think we will ever find life in space? Write two or three sentences about it.**

_____

_____

_____

_____

End of Sentence Punctuation

Different kinds of sentences end with different punctuation marks.

Kind of Sentence	End Punctuation	Example
Statement or command	Period (.)	Look at this house. It is almost 100 years old.
Question	Question mark (?)	Have you ever seen such a beautiful house?
Exclamation	Exclamation point (!)	What a beautiful house!

> **Write the appropriate end mark at the end of each sentence.**

1. Many fish live in the ocean _____

2. Do they live in the deepest waters _____

3. For the most part, they live in the middle depths _____

4. However, some live in very shallow waters _____

5. What a beautiful array of fish live on the coral reef _____

6. Look at the orange fish over there _____

7. Is that a clown fish _____

> **Rewrite the sentences on the lines. Use capital letters and end marks correctly.**

my family took a snorkeling trip on a coral reef there were so many fish have you ever been snorkeling

_____

_____

> **Revisit a piece of your writing. Edit the draft to make sure that your sentences are written with the correct punctuation.**

Capital Letters and Punctuation in Quotations

Use capital letters and punctuation to write direct quotations correctly. Always capitalize the first word of a quotation. Use a comma to separate a quotation from the words that tell who is speaking. Put punctuation inside the last quotation marks. When a quotation starts a sentence, put a comma at the end of a statement. Use the usual end punctuation for questions and exclamations.

direct quotations
Ahn exclaimed, "What a beautiful dance performance!"
"The hula is unique," Jason agreed.
"Do you think we can learn it?" asked Ahn.

> **Write the quotations correctly.**

1. Did you watch the dance Jason asked

_____

2. Ahn asked did you see the man jump over the fire

_____

3. I was afraid he was going to fall in said Jason

_____

4. I guess he must practice that dance every day said Ahn

_____

5. Jason said it's so interesting to watch different kinds of performances

_____

> **Revisit a piece of your writing. Edit the draft to make sure that your quotations are written with the correct punctuation.**

Punctuation for Effect

Punctuation can show emotion or emphasize an idea.

Ellipsis (. . .)	To show tension, threat	A strange noise came from across the room . . . what was happening?
Exclamation Point (!)	To show surprise	A painting flew off the wall and hit the floor!
Dash (—)	To emphasize	A light appeared outside—and then we heard a loud bang!

▶ **Read each sentence. Rewrite it with appropriate punctuation on the lines.**

1. Haunted houses are not real I hope

_____

2. Halloween is the perfect time to be spooked

_____

3. They told me that there is a mummy inside and I am spooked

_____

4. With the lights on, it is not scary at all

_____

5. We can't be late or we will get in trouble.

_____

▶ **Revisit a piece of your writing. Edit the draft to make sure that your sentences are written with the punctuation that creates the best effect.**

Review Punctuation

Different kinds of sentences end with different punctuation marks, including a period (.), exclamation point (!), and a question mark (?).

Punctuation can show emotion or emphasize and idea. Ellipses (. . .) show tension or a threat. Exclamation points show surprise. A dash can emphasize part of a sentence.

Always capitalize the first word of a quotation and use a comma to separate a quotation from the words that tell who is speaking. Put punctuation inside the last quotation marks.

When a quotation starts a sentence, put a comma at the end of a statement. Use the usual end punctuation for questions and exclamations.

> **Read each sentence. Rewrite it with appropriate punctuation on the line.**

1. I am so excited for our spring musical

_____

2. We all auditioned and Sarah got the lead role.

_____

3. Which is your favorite song in the musical mom asked

_____

4. I don't know I said I really like them all

_____

5. Where is your homework asked the teacher.

_____

> **Revisit a piece of your writing. Edit the draft to make sure that your sentences are written with the correct punctuation.**

Connect to Writing: Using Punctuation Correctly

> Read the selection and choose the best answer to each question.

Javier wrote the following paragraph about the spring musical his school is preparing. Read his paragraph and look for revisions he should make. Then answer the questions that follow.

(1) This spring, my school is putting on a musical? (2) We have four months to prepare, and there is so much work to do. (3) At rehearsal, the director yells, "places, everyone." (4) We rehearse until we know all the lines by heart—every day after school. (5) Everyone wonders, "Will the actors all remember their lines"? (6) On the night of the performance, the curtain fell . . . and the audience jumped to its feet, yelling, "Bravo!"

1. Which sentence is punctuated properly?

   A. This spring, my school is putting on a musical?

   B. At rehearsal, the director yells, "places, everyone."

   C. We rehearse until we know all the lines by heart—every day after school.

   D. Everyone wonders, "Will the actors all remember their lines"?

2. Which statement properly punctuates sentence 5?

   A. Everyone wonders, "Will the actors all remember their lines"?

   B. Everyone wonders, "Will the actors all remember their lines?"

   C. Everyone wonders "Will the actors all remember their lines?"

   D. Everyone wonders, "will the actors all remember their lines"?

> Have you ever seen a play or wanted to go to one? Write two or three sentences about it.

_____

_____

_____

_____

Commas with Direct Speech and Names

When you write, use a comma to set off the name of a person addressed
directly, and to set off introductory words such as *yes, no,* and *well*.

> Jack, can you tell me about the pyramids of ancient Egypt?
> Well, the most famous pyramids are around Cairo.
> I wonder, Mr. Smith, if there are pyramids outside of Egypt?

▶ **Write the sentences correctly. Add commas where they are needed.**

1. Sally did you know that the Pyramid of Khufu is the largest Egyptian pyramid?

   _____

2. No Jack I had no idea

   _____

3. The pyramids Sally were constructed from limestone.

   _____

4. Well how did they get those limestone blocks to the construction site?

   _____

5. Jack I read that the ancient Egyptians used wooden sleds to pull the blocks.

   _____

▶ **Revisit a piece of your writing. Edit the draft to make sure that you have used
commas with direct speech and names correctly.**

Commas in Compound Sentences

A **compound sentence** joins two complete ideas using a coordinating conjunction such as *and, but, or,* or *so*. Each half of a compound sentence has its own subject and predicate. Use a comma before the conjunction in a compound sentence.

subject   verb   subject verb
↓   ↓   ↓   ↓
Alligators live in swamps and rivers, **but** they sleep on land sometimes.

> **Join each pair of sentences using the conjunction in parentheses( ). Be sure your compound sentence has a comma before the conjunction.**

1. The average alligator weighs 790 pounds. They sometimes grow to over 990 pounds. (but)

   _____

2. American alligators live in many different bodies of water. Chinese alligators live only in the Yangtze River. (but)

   _____

   _____

3. Large male alligators are solitary animals. They are often found away from other alligators. (so)

   _____

4. The swamp has many alligators. People should stay away. (so)

   _____

5. At one time the American alligator was an endangered species. Today it has recovered thanks to conservation efforts. (but)

   _____

   _____

> **Revisit a piece of your writing. Edit the draft to make sure that your compound sentences use commas correctly.**

More Uses of Commas

Use a comma to separate the words in a series.

We saw <u>mockingbirds</u>, <u>hummingbirds</u>, and <u>parakeets</u> at the aviary.
There are <u>sea horses</u>, <u>shells</u>, <u>clown fish</u>, and <u>snails</u> in the aquarium.

Use a comma between a date and a year.

My birthday is <u>May 6, 2008</u>.

Use a comma between a city and a state.

I live in <u>Philadelphia</u>, <u>Pennsylvania</u>.

▶ **Add commas where they are needed. Write the sentence correctly on the line.**

1. Our annual holiday parade is on December 12 2018.

_____

2. There will be musicians firetrucks clowns and an emcee in the parade.

_____

3. The parade will start downtown in Chino California.

_____

4. Parents students teachers and visitors will attend.

_____

5. The parade will have students playing tubas drums trumpets and trombones.

_____

▶ **Revisit a piece of your writing. Edit the draft to make sure that you have used commas correctly.**

Review Commas

When you write, use a comma to set off the name of a person addressed directly, and to set off introductory words such as *yes, no,* and *well.*

Use a comma before the conjunction in a compound sentence.

Use a comma to separate the words in a series, between a date and a year, and between a city and state.

> Add commas where they are needed. Write the sentence correctly on the line.

1. Sam do you want to play basketball after school?

   _____

2. Clara Jill Jose and Anna will come to my house.

   _____

> Combine the two sentences into one using the conjunction in parentheses().
   Add commas where needed.

3. We all have homework to do. We will do our homework first. (so)

   _____

4. I want to keep playing. It is time to go home. (but)

   _____

5. We will go to the soccer game. We will go to the swim meet. (or)

   _____

> Revisit a piece of your writing. Edit the draft to make sure that you have used commas correctly.

Connect to Writing: Using Commas

> **Read the selection and choose the best answer to each question.**

Anna wrote the following paragraph about the geometry unit her class just completed. Read her paragraph and look for revisions she should make. Then answer the questions that follow.

(1) Well, we just finished our geometry unit. (2) The skills we learned are interesting useful and fun. (3) For example, you can calucuate the area of a triangle using the Pythagorean Theorem. (4) I enjoyed the unit very much. (5) I would like to learn more about geometry.

1. Which sentence above is not properly punctuated?

    A. Well, we just finished our geometry unit.

    B. The skills we learned are interesting useful and fun.

    C. For example, you can calculate the area of a triangle using the Pythagorean Theorem.

    D. I enjoyed the unit very much.

2. Which statement properly combines sentences 4 and 5?

    A. I enjoyed the unit very much? I would like to learn more about geometry!

    B. I enjoyed the unit very much, and I would like to learn more about geometry.

    C. I enjoyed the unit very much and I would like to learn more about geometry.

    D. I enjoyed the unit very much but I would like to learn more about geometry

> **What are you learning about in your favorite subject? Write two or three sentences about it.**

_____

_____

_____

_____

Name _____

Capitalization and Writing Titles

Capitalize important words in the titles of movies, books, chapters, and articles in a newspaper or magazine. Short words such as *in, if, of, a,* and *the* are not capitalized unless they are the first word in the title.

When writing the title of a shorter work, such as a story or news article, use quotation marks. When writing the title of a longer work, such as a book, magazine, or movie, underline the title.

book title
A New House for Mouse

story title
"The Travels of a Street Cat"

> **Rewrite each sentence. Add capital letters, underlining, and punctuation where they are needed.**

1. The best story in the newspaper today is which color do mice like best?

   _____

2. The phantom tollbooth is a classic novel.

   _____

3. I read a book to my sister called the best circus in the world.

   _____

4. We are reading a poem in class called jabberwocky.

   _____

5. We sang a song called All You Need.

   _____

> **Revisit a piece of your writing. Edit the draft to make sure that that your titles are capitalized and punctuated correctly.**

End Punctuation

The punctuation at the end of a sentence helps to show its meaning. Use a period (.) at the end of a statement or a command. Use a question mark (?) at the end of a question and an exclamation point (!) to show strong feeling.

declarative	I enjoy reading.
imperative	Pass me that book, please.
interrogative	What is the title of your book?
exclamatory	What a great story!

> Add the correct end mark for each sentence. Write *declarative, interrogative, imperative,* or *exclamatory* on the line.

1. Our library has so many great books _____

2. Do you want to go to the library after school _____

3. You must read A Wrinkle in Time _____

4. Madeline L'Engle is such a great writer _____

5. We read Wonder in class this year _____

6. When I'm bored, I read a good book _____

7. Why don't you try the new book about robots _____

8. Give it to me when you are finished with it _____

9. There are many books I want to read _____

10. Let's read a book together _____

> Revisit a piece of your writing. Edit the draft to make sure that all of your sentences have the correct end punctuation.

Commas Before Coordinating Conjunctions

> A **compound sentence** joins two independent clauses using the coordinating conjunctions *and, but, or, nor, for,* or *so*. Use a comma before the conjunction.
>
> The children were curious about the book, <u>for</u> they had never seen one.
>
> Children can learn in a classroom, <u>or</u> they can learn through computer lessons.

▷ **Join each pair of sentences to make a compound sentence using the conjunction shown in parentheses. Use commas correctly.**

1. Robots can be controlled by an external device. They can be controlled from within. (or)

   _____

2. Some robots do jobs that are unsafe for humans. Some robots do jobs that are in extreme environments. (and)

   _____

   _____

3. Most robots work in factories. Some robots work deep underwater. (but)

   _____

4. Robots don't have feelings. They will never replace humans. (so)

   _____

5. Robots are not creative. They cannot give advice. (and)

   _____

▷ **Revisit a piece of your writing. Edit the draft to make sure that you have placed commas correctly before coordinating conjunctions.**

Review Proper Mechanics

Capitalize important words in the titles of movies, books, chapters, and articles in a newspaper or magazine. Short words such as *in*, *if*, *of*, *a*, and *the* are not capitalized unless they are the first word in the title.

When writing the title of a shorter work, such as a story or news article, use quotation marks. When writing the title of a longer work, such as a book, magazine, or movie, underline the title.

Use a period (.) at the end of a statement or a command. Use a question mark (?) at the end of a question and an exclamation point (!) to show strong feeling.

A **compound sentence** joins two independent clauses using the coordinating conjunctions *and*, *but*, *or*, *nor*, *for*, or *so*. Use a comma before the conjunction.

▶ **Rewrite each sentence using capital letters, underlining, commas, and other punctuation as needed.**

1. You can see photographs of other cultures in national geographic

_____

2. Would you like to travel to Marrakesh Morocco

_____

3. The photographs in the article entitled a village by the sea are beautiful

_____

▶ **Combine the pairs of sentences to make a compound sentence using the conjunction shown in parentheses. Use commas correctly.**

4. I'm going to pack many items. I need an extra suitcase. (so)

_____

5. We've traveled all day. We are exhausted. (and)

_____

Connect to Writing: Using Proper Mechanics

> **Read the selection and choose the best answer to each question.**

Hassan wrote the following paragraph about a conversation he had with his friends about his travels. Read his paragraph and look for revisions he should make. Then answer the questions that follow.

(1) When my family decided to go to France, we borrowed a travel guide from the library. (2) It had a travel article called hiking from mountain to sea. (3) Why hadn't we thought about hiking on our trip! (4) We decided to bring backpacks. (5) We also packed hiking boots.

1. Which statement below properly punctuates statement 2?

   A. It had a travel article called Hiking from Mountain to Sea.

   B. It had a travel article called Hiking from Mountain to Sea.

   C. It had a travel article called "Hiking From Mountain To Sea."

   D. It had a travel article called "Hiking from Mountain to Sea."

2. Which statement properly combines statements 4 and 5?

   A. We decided to bring backpacks so we also packed hiking boots.

   B. We decided to bring backpacks, and we also packed hiking boots.

   C. We decided to bring backpacks we also packed hiking boots.

   D. We decided to bring backpacks but we also packed hiking boots.

> **Have you ever been hiking? Write two or three sentences about it.**

_____

_____

_____

_____

To, Too, and Two

Do not confuse the words *to, too,* and *two*. They sound the same, but they have different spellings and meanings.

to means "in the direction of"	I ran **to** the finish line.
too means "also" or "in addition"	I wanted an ice cream cone, **too**.
two is a number	There are **two** scoops on my cone.

> **Complete each sentence with *to, too,* or *two,* as appropriate.**

1. There are _____ ice cream shops in my town.

2. I like strawberry, but I like vanilla, _____.

3. My sister said she'd take me _____ the movies with her.

4. My friend Ben has _____ sisters.

5. They want ice cream, _____.

> **Revisit a piece of your writing. Edit the draft to make sure that you have used the correct form of *to, two,* or *too*.**

There, They're, and Their

Do not confuse the words *there, they're,* and *their*. They sound the same, but they have different spellings and meanings.

there means "in that place"	We ran over **there** to get out of the rain.
they're is a contraction of *they are*	**They're** wearing raincoats.
their means "belonging to them"	They didn't bring **their** umbrellas.

> **Complete each sentence with *there, they're,* or *their*.**

1. My friends Sally and Eve lent us _____ sleds.

2. _____ on their way out of town for the weekend.

3. Several inches of snow fell _____ last night.

4. It seems like the snow _____ is deep enough to go sledding.

5. "Be careful sledding," said _____ father.

> **Revisit a piece of your writing. Edit the draft to make sure that you are using the correct form of *there, their,* or *they're*.**

Its and *It's*

Do not confuse the words *its* and *it's*. They sound the same, but they have different spellings and meanings.

its means "belonging to it"	The team carried <u>its</u> trophy around the field.
it's is a contraction of *it is* or *it has*	<u>It's</u> been awhile since they won.

> **Complete each sentence with *its* or *it's*.**

1. The team won _____ game today.

2. _____ a good thing, because they were close to being eliminated.

3. My uncle said _____ been five years since the team had a winning record.

4. The team had sent all of _____ equipment to the storage room.

5. The mascot wore _____ costume to school the next day.

> **Revisit a piece of your writing. Edit the draft to make sure that you are using the correct form of *its* and *it's*.**

Review Frequently Confused Words

Do not confuse the words *its* and *it's*; *they're*, *their*, and *there*; and *to*, *too*, and *two*. They sound the same, but they have different spellings and meanings.

▶ **Complete each sentence with the correct form of the word in parentheses.**

1. (It's, Its) (to, too, two) soon to worry about how we are going to get (there, their, they're). _____

2. (There, They're, Their) car is good for a long trip, because (its, it's) trunk is big. _____

3. (Its, It's) a good thing the roof rack can hold all of (there, they're, their) extra baggage. _____

4. The team packed all of (its, it's) equipment in the other van. _____

5. I think we are going to need more than (to, too, two) cars to bring all the stuff (their, there, they're) packing. _____

▶ **Revisit a piece of your writing. Edit the draft to make sure that you have used the correct form of the words.**

Connect to Writing: Using the Correct Word

> Read the selection and choose the best answer to each question.

Penelope wrote the following paragraph about her plans to go skiing over the winter break. Read her paragraph and look for revisions she should make. Then, answer the questions that follow.

(1) Penelope and her family packed they're skiis and cold weather clothes for a ski trip. (2) Their had been several snowstorms. (3) The mountain had at least too feet of snow. (4) The ski lodge had its fireplace repaired. (5) A fire was burning to warm their hands and feet after a long day of skiing.

1. What change should be made to Sentence 2?

   A. Change *Their* to *They're.*

   B. Change *Their* to *Thier.*

   C. Change *Their* to *There.*

   D. Make no change.

2. Which statement is written correctly??

   A. Penelope and her family packed they're skiis and cold weather clothes for a ski trip.

   B. The mountain had at least too feet of snow.

   C. The ski lodge had its fireplace repaired.

   D. A fire was burning to warm there hands and feet after a long day of skiing.

> What activities do you like to do in the cold weather? Write two or three sentences about it.

_____

_____

_____

_____

_____

Abbreviations for People and Places

An abbreviation is a short form of a word. Most abbreviations begin with a capital letter and end with a period. Both letters of state name abbreviations are capital letters, and no period is used.

Person	Mrs. Sally Stevens
Place	28 East Rd.
Place	Winklet, VA 40597

> **Write each group of words. Use an abbreviation for the underlined word or words.**

1. Klackett Drum <u>Company</u> _____

2. Ken Kelson, <u>Junior</u> _____

3. 47 Radio <u>Lane</u> _____

4. <u>Doctor</u> Steve Steinson _____

5. 469 Waverly <u>Boulevard</u> _____

6. <u>Mister</u> Jasper Trillings, <u>Senior</u> _____

7. 589 Ocean <u>Drive</u> _____

8. Shilling, <u>Texas</u> 84702 _____

9. <u>Missus</u> Jane Lee _____

10. New Providence, <u>New Jersey</u> 07974 _____

> **Revisit a piece of your writing. Edit the draft to make sure that you have used abbreviations correctly.**

Abbreviations for Mailing Addresses

An abbreviation is a short form of a word. Use abbreviations when writing street names and states in a mailing address. Abbreviate words such as road or avenue with a capital letter and end with a period. Write both letters of state name abbreviations with capital letters and do not use periods.

Road	Rd.	Court	Ct.
Street	St.	Post Office	P.O.
Avenue	Ave.	Boulevard	Blvd.

▶ **Write each mailing address using abbreviations.**

Full Address	Abbreviated Address
1. Mister David Jones 368 Southwest Lane Missoula, Montana 59827	
2. Matthew Westerly, Junior Post Office Box 5398 Portland, Maine 02997	
3. Missus Mary Maint President, Executive Corporation 7400 Corporate Lane West Overly, New Hampshire 09371	

▶ **Revisit a piece of your writing. Edit the draft to make sure that you have used abbreviations correctly.**

Abbreviations for Time and Measurement

An abbreviation is a short form of a word. The abbreviations for days and months begin with a capital letter and end with a period. Some other abbreviations for time and measurements begin with a lowercase letter and end with a period.

time
6 hr., 27 min.

measurement
165 mi., 4 yd.

> **Write these groups of word using correct abbreviations.**

1. 7,000 feet _____

2. 2 hours, 15 minutes _____

3. Monday, February 8, 2010 _____

4. Friday – Sunday _____

5. 5 yards, 8 inches _____

6. September 26, 1987 _____

7. December 24, 2003 _____

8. Tuesday, March 31, 1776 _____

9. 4 hours, 10 minutes _____

10. October 17, 1954 _____

> **Revisit a piece of your writing. Edit the draft to make sure that you have used abbreviations for time, dates, and measurements correctly.**

Review Abbreviations

Both letters of state name abbreviations are capital letters, and no period is used.

Use abbreviations when writing street names and states in a mailing address. Abbreviate words such as road or avenue with a capital letter and end with a period.

The abbreviations for days and months begin with a capital letter and end with a period. Some other abbreviations for time and measurements begin with a lowercase letter and end with a period.

▷ **Write these groups of words using correct abbreviations.**

1. Mister Harry Bradley _____

2. 7 hours, 17 minutes _____

3. 237 East Jefferson Street _____

4. Post Office Box 318 _____

5. September 4, 1980 _____

6. Stephen Andrews, Senior _____

7. October 24, 1888 _____

8. Tuesday – Friday _____

9. 4 miles _____

10. Doctor Yves Mclean _____

▷ **Revisit a piece of your writing. Edit the draft to make sure that you have used abbreviations correctly.**

Connect to Writing: Using Abbreviations

> **Read the selection and choose the best answer to each question.**
Clara wrote the following paragraph about her family's plan to move to a different city. Read her paragraph and look for revisions she should make. Then answer the questions that follow.

(1) Clara's father, Doctor Chad Wexler, got a new job. (2) He told the family they would have to move to Omaha, Nebraska. (3) They sold their house at 365 East Main Street in Houston, Texas. (4) They drove 659 miles to Omaha. (5) They moved into their new house at 59 Strawson Lane.

1. Which is abbreviated correctly?

 A. He told the family they would have to move to Omaha, NE.

 B. He told the family they would have to move to Om., Nebraska.

 C. He told the family they would have to move to Omaha, Nebraska.

 D. He told the family they would have to move to Omaha, NB.

2. Which is abbreviated correctly?

 A. They sold their house at 365 East Main St. in Houston, Texas.

 B. They sold their house at 365 East Main St. in Houston, TX.

 C. They sold their house at 365 East Main Street in Houston, TE.

 D. They sold their house at 365 East Main Street in Hou., Texas.

> **Have you ever moved to a new town or city? If not, would you like to? Write two or three sentences about it.**

_____

_____

_____

_____

Spelling Homophones

> Sometimes two words that sound alike are spelled differently and have different meanings. These words are called **homophones**.
>
> • Some examples of commonly used homophones are: *their/there/they're, its/it's,* and *too/to/two.*

> Complete the sentences using the correct homophone in parentheses.

1. Wake up—(its, it's) time to go! _____

2. The team members wore (they're, there, their) jerseys to the parade. _____

3. I'm on my way (to, two, too) the library. _____

4. The treehouse is in the tree over (their, there, they're). _____

5. She told me (their, there, they're) planning to leave at noon. _____

6. There are (to, too, two) reasons I want to go on the trip. _____

7. The tree is dropping (its, it's) leaves. _____

8. I told my sister that she could come, (to, two, too). _____

9. We want (to, two) ice cream cones today. _____

10. They left (their, there, they're) umbrellas inside. _____

> Revisit a piece of your writing. Edit the draft to make sure that you have used the correct homophone.

Spelling Words with Endings

Adding the ending -s to a singular noun will change it to a plural noun. If the word ends with s, x, z, sh, or ch, add -es. If the word ends with y, change the y to i and add -es.

Add the endings -ed or -ing to verbs to change their tense. If the word ends with e, drop the e before adding the ending. If the final letters are a short vowel followed by a single consonant, double the consonant before adding the ending.

> John has two <u>violins</u>.
> We are <u>studying</u> for the test.
> I <u>studied</u> for the math test last night.

> **Rewrite the sentences making the changes to the underlined word based on the instruction in parentheses.**

1. I <u>clean</u> the house on Sundays. (past) _____

2. Sarah has one <u>cat</u>. (plural) _____

3. We <u>hurry</u> along the path to school. (past) _____

4. Jackson has one <u>box</u>. (plural) _____

5. I <u>washed</u> the dishes last night. (present) _____

> **Revisit a piece of your writing. Edit the draft to make sure that your word endings are correct.**

Spelling Words with Suffixes

A **suffix** is a word part that is added to the end of a **root** word to change its meaning.

Commonly used suffixes include: -ful, -less, -sion, -tion, -able, -ible

She was <u>careless</u> and got several answers wrong.

That teddy bear is <u>loveable</u>!

> Add a suffix to the underlined word in each sentence.

1. It was <u>thought</u> of her to forget Sarah's birthday. _____

2. That wood is easy to use because it is <u>ply</u>. _____

3. Don't be <u>care</u> when reviewing your essay. _____

4. This pot roast is <u>wonder</u>. _____

5. The room was full of <u>tense</u>. _____

> Revisit a piece of your writing. Edit the draft to make sure that your suffixes are written correctly.

Review Spelling

Sometimes two words that sound alike are spelled differently and have different meanings. These words are called **homophones**.

Add the ending -s to a singular noun to change it to a plural noun. Add the endings -ed or -ing to verbs to change their tense.

Adding a suffix to the end of a word changes the meaning of the word.

▷ Choose the correct homophone in parentheses to complete the sentence.

1. Please (write, right) to me every day! _____

2. Her house is over (there, their, they're). _____

3. I'm taking a trip to the (see, sea). _____

▷ Write the plural form of the underlined noun.

4. Steve has six <u>basketball</u>. _____

5. There are seven <u>fox</u> over there. _____

6. There are nine <u>fish</u> in the tank. _____

▷ Add the correct suffix to the underlined word.

7. The garden was <u>bounty</u> this year. _____

8. The broken scissors are <u>use</u>. _____

9. She needs to have an <u>operate</u> to remove her tonsils. _____

10. The librarian was very <u>help</u>. _____

▷ Revisit a piece of your writing. Edit the draft to make sure that your words are spelled correctly.

_____

Grade 4 • Frequently Misspelled Words

Connect to Writing: Use Correct Spelling

> **Read the selection and choose the best answer to each question.**

Steve wrote the following paragraph about the games he plays with his friends at school. Read his paragraph and look for revisions he should make. Then answer the questions that follow.

     (1) We often played kickball at recess. (2) The pitcher careful rolls the ball to the kicker. (3) The kicker run around the bases. (4) After one our of recess we go to lunch. (5) We sit at long tables in the cafeteria.

1. Which sentence above is correct?

   A. We often played kickball at recess.

   B. The pitcher careful rolls the ball to the kicker.

   C. The kicker run around the bases.

   D. We sit at long tables in the cafeteria.

2. Which statement is the properly edited version of sentence 1?

   A. We often plays kickball at recess.

   B. We often play kickball at recess.

   C. We of ten played kickball at recess.

   D. We often playing kickball at recess.

> **What do you and your friends play at recess? Write two or three sentences about it.**

_____

_____

_____

_____